PCs Just the Steps™
FOR
DUMMIES®

by Nancy Muir

WILEY

Wiley Publishing, Inc.

PCs Just the Steps™ For Dummies®

Published by
Wiley Publishing, Inc.
111 River Street
Hoboken, NJ 07030-5774
www.wiley.com

For general information on our other products and services, please contact our Customer Care Department within the U.S. at 800-762-2974, outside the U.S. at 317-572-3993, or fax 317-572-4002.

For technical support, please visit www.wiley.com/techsupport.

Wiley also publishes its books in a variety of electronic formats. Some content that appears in print may not be available in electronic books.

Library of Congress Control Number: 2005937345

ISBN-13: 978-0-471-75794-8
ISBN-10: 0-471-75794-2

Manufactured in the United States of America

10 9 8 7 6 5 4 3 2 1

1B/RU/QS/QW/IN

WILEY

About the Author

Nancy Muir has written over 50 books on technology and business topics (many under her previous name of Nancy Stevenson). She is the author of *Distance Learning Online For Dummies, Microsoft Project For Dummies,* and *Windows XP Just the Steps For Dummies* as well as numerous other titles for a variety of publishers. She has a certificate in distance learning design and has taught technical writing at the university level. She lives with her wonderful family in Washington (state), where she acts in plays, sings, walks (a lot!), and occasionally writes a novel.

Dedication

This is the first book I will have published after recently getting married, so I want to dedicate this one to my new husband, Earl, for being such a wonderful partner. He truly is my soul mate, and his support, love, sense of humor, and sense of joy imbue all my days with happiness (even those days with book deadlines!).

Author's Acknowledgments

Thanks, as always, to Wiley for wanting to work with me, and to Andy Cummings and Mary Bednarek for their friendship over the years. Thanks also to Greg Croy for continuing to hire me for book projects. My heartfelt thanks to Blair Pottenger for being such a delight to work with and for making my scribblings intelligible (even while planning for his own wedding — congratulations Blair and Carol!). The efforts of Lee Musick as technical editor and Teresa Artman as copy editor also are a major factor in the accuracy and readability of this book.

Publisher's Acknowledgments

We're proud of this book; please send us your comments through our online registration form located at www.dummies.com/register/. Some of the people who helped bring this book to market include the following:

Acquisitions, Editorial, and Media Development

Project Editor: Blair J. Pottenger

Executive Editor: Gregory Croy

Senior Copy Editor: Teresa Artman

Technical Editor: Lee Musick

Editorial Manager: Kevin Kirschner

Editorial Assistant: Amanda Foxworth

Cartoons: Rich Tennant (www.the5thwave.com)

Composition Services

Project Coordinator: Adrienne Martinez

Layout and Graphics: Lauren Goddard, Denny Hager, Lynsey Osborn, Heather Ryan, Erin Zeltner

Proofreaders: Leeann Harney, Betty Kish, Jessica Kramer

Indexer: Johnna VanHoose

Publishing and Editorial for Technology Dummies

Richard Swadley, Vice President and Executive Group Publisher

Andy Cummings, Vice President and Publisher

Mary Bednarek, Executive Acquisitions Director

Mary C. Corder, Editorial Director

Publishing for Consumer Dummies

Diane Graves Steele, Vice President and Publisher

Joyce Pepple, Acquisitions Director

Composition Services

Gerry Fahey, Vice President of Production Services

Debbie Stailey, Director of Composition Services

Contents at a Glance

I'm guessing you don't put computer books at the top of your summer reading list. When you need a computer book, you don't want to wade through a tome just to be able to get to work on your computer. You just want to get in, find out how to do something, and get out. You're not alone. I was delighted to write a book where I could get right to the details of how to do things — and move on. None of that telling you what I'm going to say, saying it, and then reviewing what I just said. That's why I was happy to write a *Just the Steps For Dummies* book about PCs.

About This Book

Today's PC is a pretty sophisticated piece of hardware, with about as much functionality as a rocketship. If you own a Windows-based computer (and I assume you do, or you should pass this book on to somebody who does), you spend a lot of time every day on your computer. Knowing how to harness the power of your hardware and software is what this book is all about. As the title suggests, I give you just the steps you need to do many of the most common PC-related tasks. This book is all about getting productive right away.

Note that this book is based on the Windows XP version of the operating system. If you have an earlier or later version, some procedures and the screens you see may differ.

Why You Need This Book

You can't wait weeks to learn how to use your computer or to fix a problem when it occurs. Your computer is a piece of hardware where all your software lives: how you get to your e-mail and documents. You have to manage both everyday tasks and emergency situations quickly. When you hit a bump in the road, whether caused by your hardware or software, you need a quick answer to get you moving again. This book is full of quick, clear steps that keep you computing rather than reading.

Introduction

Conventions used in this book

➡ When you have to type something in a text box, I put it in **bold** type.

➡ For menu commands, I use the ➪ symbol to separate menu items: for example, choose Tools➪Internet Options. The ➪ symbol is just my way of saying "Choose Internet Options from the Tools menu."

➡ Points of interest in some figures are circled. The text tells you what to look for, and the circle makes it easy to find.

 This icon points out insights or helpful suggestions related to tasks in the step list.

How This Book Is Organized

This book is conveniently divided into several handy parts:

Part I: Hardware Basics

Here's where you discover the various elements of a PC system, from the CPU to peripherals (such as printers) as well as input devices. You find the best way to hook things up and use various settings to make them all run happily and efficiently.

Part II: The Brains of the Beast

Windows XP — your operating system — controls a wealth of functionality on your PC. You want Windows XP to function in a way that matches your style, right? This is the part where you explore how to work in the Windows' XP environment, customize its behavior, and organize your files and folders.

Part III: Working with Your Display, Multimedia, and Graphics

Your monitor is your entrée into the world of your computer. Getting your view set just right involves adjustments to the monitor itself as well as working with various video and display settings. This is the part where you get your display set up just as you want it.

Part IV: Going Online

The whole world is online, and you can't be any exception. Here's where I show you how to connect, how to browse, and how to do e-mail.

Part V: Networking

More and more people are discovering the convenience of being able to network two or more computers to share files, an Internet connection, or a printer. Setting up a network of your own isn't all that hard, and you can read all about it right here. Whether you want a network that involves plugging in cables, or you are ready to enter the world of wireless connections, you will find help in these chapters.

Part VI: Security and Troubleshooting

Yes, I admit: Your PC can have problems. Some of those problems relate to protecting your system from intruders, while others spring from hardware or software glitches. Luckily, Windows XP also has tools to keep you — or get you — out of trouble. In this part, I explain how to make your computer secure and how to deal with hardware and software problems.

Get Ready To . . .

Whether you just need to plug in a new printer and get printing, check your e-mail, or make the most of your computer memory, just browse this book, pick a task, and jump in. Your PC can be your best friend if you know how to use it, and the tasks covered in this book will make you a PC pro in no time.

Part I
Hardware Basics

The 5th Wave   By Rich Tennant

"That reminds me – I have to figure out how to install our CD-ROM and external hard drive."

First Look at Your PC

Your desktop computer might be a big tower, or perhaps it's built into a single unit with your monitor. It likely has multiple slots and places to plug in things *(ports)* as well as indicator lights that tell you what's working and what's not.

When you get your PC out of the box, you'll probably find a handy document showing you just where to plug in things, such as your monitor, keyboard, and mouse. Today's computers often color-code plugs, so it's easy to spot where a particular item plugs in. Still, a basic overview of what's on your PC, how you turn your computer on and off, and how you get around the Windows XP desktop is helpful to many people. And although all computer models differ somewhat, the information and illustrations in this chapter should help you locate various switches and connectors on your own computer.

If you have never handled a PC before, use the tasks in this chapter to do the following:

➡ **Locate connections on the front and back of your computer:** You use these connections to connect your monitor, printer, mouse, keyboard, and more.

➡ **Turn on your computer, get around the Windows XP desktop, and turn off your computer:** This is your first introduction to booting up, using, and logging off your computer.

Chapter

1

Get ready to . . .

Locate Switches and Plug In Things

Use this table in tandem with Figure 1-1 to help you locate device-to-PC connector ports.

Connection	Location	What It's Good For
Mouse	1	Connect your wired mouse
Serial port	2	Connect your monitor
Keyboard	3	Connect your wired keyboard
USB port	4	Connect various USB devices, such as a digital camera
Parallel port	5	Connect a non-USB printer
Audio	6	Connect speakers
Joystick port	7	Connect a joystick input device

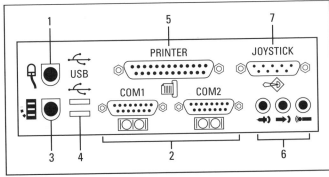

Figure 1-1: Various places to plug things into your PC

Note that some monitors and laptop computers have built in speakers so that you don't need to connect separate speakers through the audio port. Discover more about working with sound settings in Chapter 13.

Not every computer will have the same number or type of ports. For example, a laptop may only have a USB port for a printer and not a parallel port. Some computers have two USB ports while others have 4 or 5. Over time, the tendency will be to have USB but not serial or parallel ports, as most monitors and printers being manufactured today use the USB connection type.

Turn On Your PC and Log In

1. Press the Power button. Your computer starts up, displaying a series of screens until you observe one of two possible results:

   • You reach the Windows XP log-on screen, as shown in Figure 1-2, listing all users of this computer. Click the icon for the user you want to log on as.

   • If you have only one user on this computer, you are taken directly to the Windows XP desktop.

 To log out from one user and log in as another, choose Start➪Log Off. This takes you to a Log Off window, where you can click the Switch button to log in with a different user's settings.

 If you have set a password for accessing Windows XP, you log on a bit differently. See Chapter 7 for more about this procedure.

 If this is the very first time you've turned on your computer out of the box, your manufacturer may have included an introductory series of screens to make certain settings for how your computer will work. See your computer documentation for working with any such program.

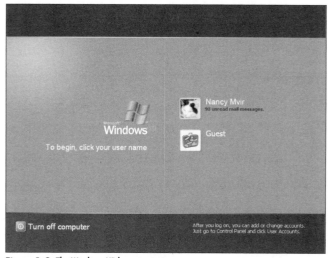

Figure 1-2: The Windows XP log-on screen

Turn Off Your PC

1. Choose Start⇨Turn Off Computer.

2. In the resulting Turn Off Computer window, as shown in Figure 1-3, click Turn Off. Windows XP closes, and the computer turns off.

 You can also choose Restart to turn off and then immediately turn on your computer. You would use this setting if your computer is having problems and you want your system to reset, or if you install new software or make new settings and are instructed to restart your computer.

 The Standby option in the Turn Off Computer window is like letting your computer take a nap. The screen goes dark, and in the case of laptops power consumption lowers. By clicking your mouse or pressing Enter on your keyboard you can wake it up again with everything just as you left it.

 When you turn off your computer, peripherals such as your monitor or printer don't turn off automically. You have to press their power buttons to turn each off manually.

Figure 1-3: The Turn Off Computer screen

Navigate the Windows XP Desktop

1. With the Windows XP desktop displayed (see Figure 1-4), do any of the following:

   • Double-click a shortcut item to open that program, folder, or document.

   • Right-click an item to display a shortcut menu for commonly performed tasks such as Open, Send To, or Copy.

   • Right-click the desktop area to display a shortcut menu for tasks related to organizing the desktop.

2. Move your mouse to the bottom of the screen to display the Windows XP taskbar (see Figure 1-5) if it's not already displayed. Do any of the following:

   • Click a window button for a running application to maximize it.

   • Click items in the system tray to see the current date/time, or access other special Windows XP programs. Some items here just display information when you hover your mouse over them, others you can double-click to open a window with more options or information.

   • Click a button on the Quick Launch bar to start various programs.

   • Click the Start button to open the Start menu. (See next task for more information.)

 Windows XP has some preset desktop icons, such as the Recycle Bin (used to store deleted files), and your computer manufacturer probably placed several icons on the desktop for preinstalled programs. You can also create your own shortcuts; see Chapter 7 for more about how to do this.

Figure 1-4: The Windows XP desktop

Figure 1-5: The Windows XP taskbar

Use the Start Menu

1. Choose Start from the Windows XP taskbar.

2. In the resulting Start menu, as shown in Figure 1-6, do any of the following:

   • Click a frequently used program in the top left pane.

   • Click a recently used program in the middle left pane.

   • Click frequently used folders in the top right pane.

   • Click useful utilities and settings in the middle and bottom panes on the right.

   • Click All Programs in the bottom left pane, and then choose an installed program to open from the menu that appears (see Figure 1-7). When you click a program listed here, it either opens or displays a submenu with additional choices.

 You can modify the programs that are listed in the Start menu. Just right-click the Start menu area and then choose Properties. In the Properties dialog box that appears, click the Customize button for the Start menu and make various settings to how many programs and which programs appear by default.

Figure 1-6: The Start Menu

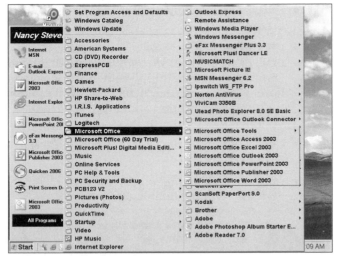

Figure 1-7: The All Programs submenu

Using Discs and Drives

*T*he *motherboard* of your computer is where all the circuitry for your PC lives. The motherboard also contains the processor chip that runs your computer. Your hard drive is also connected to the motherboard. This hard drive (typically designated as the C drive) is the main physical storage area for a PC.

You can also use removable media drives — such as a floppy drive, CD-ROM drive, a DVD drive, or a Zip drive — to give the motherboard access to additional data. Your computer can then read files from that media as well as write files to it. You can also attach an external drive to your computer for even more storage options.

Of course, you need a way to view and work with all that data, wherever it is stored. In this chapter, you explore your drives, inserting and ejecting disk/cs, and locating drive and disk/c contents and properties.

Get ready to . . .

Insert and Eject a CD-ROM or DVD Disc

1. Locate the drive (see Figure 2-1) and push the button next to it to open it.

2. Place the disc into the drive and push it shut manually or by pushing the button next to the drive.

3. To eject the disc, choose Start⇨My Computer.

4. In the resulting My Computer window, shown in Figure 2-2, right-click a disc and choose Eject. The disc drive opens so that you can remove the disc.

5. Close the drive.

 Your PC is flexible when it comes to drives. You can also use the method for ejecting your disc to open the disc drive rather than pushing the button to open it, or use the manual method of pushing the button on the closed drive to eject the disc.

 If you have a floppy drive or a zip drive, these work pretty much the same except that instead of a CD-ROM holder sliding out for you to place a disc on or remove a disc from, the actual floppy or zip disk pops out of or slips into a slot in your computer.

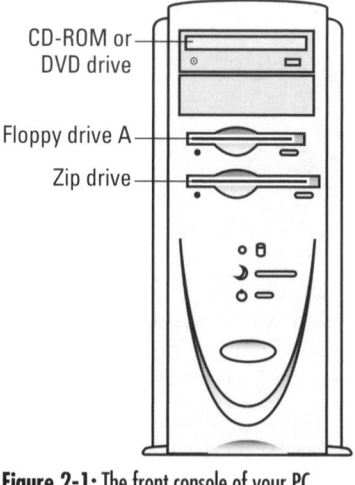

Figure 2-1: The front console of your PC

CD-ROM or DVD drive

Floppy drive A

Zip drive

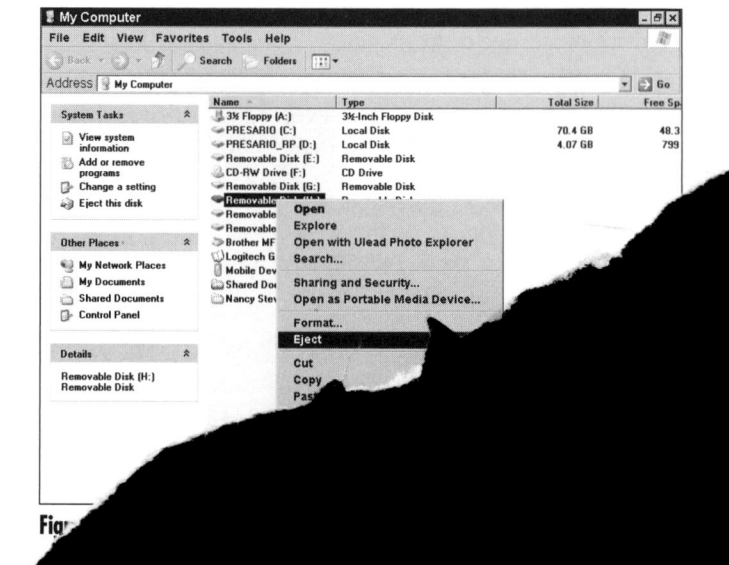

Fig

View Drive Contents

1. Choose Start➪My Computer.

2. In the resulting My Computer window, double-click your hard drive (usually C) or any other drive letter where files and folders are stored (for example, D for a CD-ROM). The contents of your drive display (see Figure 2-3), including both folders and individual files. (See Chapter 10 for more about working with folders and files.)

3. Now you can do either of the following:

   • Double-click a folder to display its contents.

   • Double-click a file to open it in the application where it was created or in a program that has been associated with it (for example, Windows Fax and Picture Viewer if it's a graphics file).

4. Click the Close button to close the window.

 Your manufacturer might have named your hard drive after your computer model. For example, my Compaq displays Presario (C:) in the My Computer window. Just look for the C part, and you'll be fine.

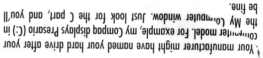 You can also view contents of folders on your computer using Windows Explorer. Choose Start➪All Programs➪Accessories➪Windows Explorer. Click the Up arrow to move up through the folders to find the My Computer window.

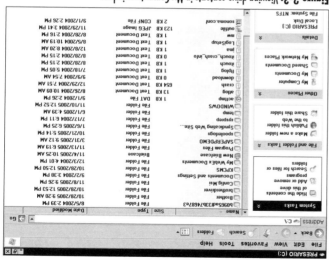

Figure 2-3: Viewing drive contents in My Computer window

Check Your Hard Drive Properties

1. Choose Start⇨My Computer.

2. In the My Computer window, as shown in Figure 2-4, right-click your hard drive and choose Properties.

3. In the Properties dialog box that appears (see Figure 2-5), locate the Used Space and Free Space information on the General tab. This tells you the amount of available space for programs and files on your hard drive.

4. Click OK or Cancel to close the dialog box.

If you have very little hard drive space left, you can perform certain maintenance tasks to free some space. See Chapter 8 for more about managing memory on your computer.

One option in the hard drive Properties dialog box is to Allow Indexing Service to index this disk for fast file searching. This is selected by default. This is the feature that allows you to search for files by properties such as date created, as well as making searches run a bit faster. I recommend leaving it turned on.

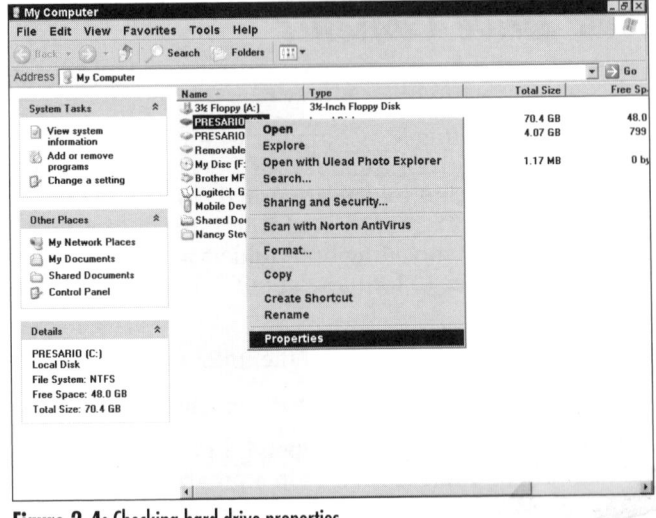

Figure 2-4: Checking hard drive properties

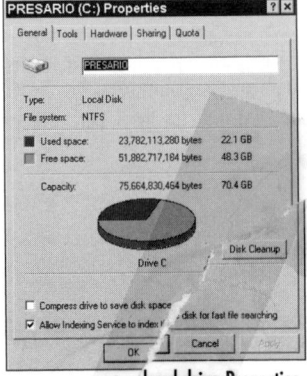

Figure 2-5: The hard drive Properties dialog box

Add an External Drive

1. Locate the USB port on the back or front of your computer (see Figure 2-6) and have a USB cable ready. Check your drive's documentation for instructions on installing any software prior to connecting the device.

2. Plug the external drive into the port by plugging the B connector into the drive and the A connector into the PC (see Figure 2-7).

3. A small pop-up should appear on your taskbar indicating that Windows XP detected the new drive. Windows XP should automatically detect the device, and you're ready to use it. If Windows XP doesn't handle this automatically, see Chapter 3 for more about installing a hardware driver.

If you don't have a USB port, you can add an external drive to the printer port. However, you can connect only one device to the port, so if it's already taken, you're out of luck. In that case, consider buying a USB expansion card for your PC — it's worth having!

Just because you have plenty of drive storage space, don't think you don't need to back up anymore. Both internal and external drives eventually fail, so be sure to back up to some other media on a regular basis.

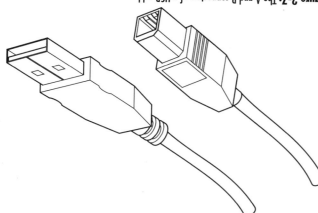

Figure 2-6: A USB port on a PC

Figure 2-7: The A and B connectors of a USB cable

Working with Input Devices

All the data and graphics stored on your computer drives are dandy, but unless you can manipulate them, they won't do you much good. That's where input devices come in. You plug *input devices* into your PC (or with a wireless device, plug in a USB transmitter) and then use them to enter data into, edit, and generally work with electronic files and even play games. You're likely to use a few different types of input devices. In this chapter, I tell you how to set up your

➡ **Keyboard:** Like typewriters of old, you type on a keyboard to enter text in a document, whether it's a word-processed letter, a spreadsheet, or a slide presentation. But computer keyboards go further than a typewriter because you can use certain key combinations — *shortcuts* — to do a wide variety of editing and formatting actions, such as cutting/pasting objects or selected text or changing how text looks.

➡ **Mouse:** A mouse is a more tactile kind of input device. Whether it comes in the form of a laptop touchpad, a mouse you move around your desk, or a trackball device, the basic purpose of a mouse is to move an onscreen cursor that allows you to select objects or text, click and drag objects within a document, or right-click an object to display shortcut menus.

➡ **Game controller:** Some models are referred to as *joysticks,* and some are *game pads.* The sole purpose of these little guys is to allow you to interact with computer games, moving among space aliens, blitzing bad guys into the ether, and the like.

Identify Different Types of Input Devices

Use this table in tandem with Figure 3-1 and Figure 3-2 to help you identify the different types of input devices.

Device	What It's Good For
Mouse	Select text and objects, click and drag to move things, display shortcut menus
Keyboard	Enter text and numbers, access shortcuts for common actions
Game controller	Maneuver around games, shoot bad guys

 Some PC devices, such as the Tablet PC, also accept input through a touch screen. By using a stylus, you can tap to make selections or write directly on the screen. If you're lucky enough to have one of these fun gadgets, beware: Use only the stylus that came with the device to touch the screen, or you could damage the screen!

 Wireless devices should just about all be Plug and Play, which means that Windows XP should detect and set them up for you as soon as you plug the wireless receiver into a USB port. If the device isn't detected or set up automatically, perhaps you need to install some associated software first. Or, follow the New Hardware Setup Wizard, as described in Chapter 5.

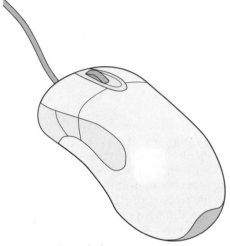

Figure 3-1: The standard PC mouse

Figure 3-2: The standard 104-key keyboard

Set Up Your Mouse

1. Choose Start⇨Control Panel⇨Printers and Other Hardware. In the resulting Printers and Other Hardware window, as shown in Figure 3-3, click the Mouse link.

2. In the resulting Mouse Properties dialog box, click the Motion tab, as shown in Figure 3-4. Then do any of the following:

   - Click and drag the Speed slider to adjust how quickly the mouse cursor moves across your computer screen.

   - Click to enable or disable *Smart Move,* which causes your mouse cursor to automatically move to the button that's highlighted in any dialog box.

   - Click to enable or disable *cursor trails,* which are essentially shadows that follow your cursor as it moves across the screen. You can also use the Trail Length slider to adjust whether you see a looooong or short tail.

3. Click OK to apply your changes and close the dialog box.

 You can use settings on the Pointers tab of the Mouse Properties dialog box to change the icons used for different cursors. For example, you could change the normal cursor arrow to a dinosaur or metronome. Should you? Why not? But remember that such changes could be confusing to anybody else who uses your computer.

 Use the Buttons tab of the Mouse Properties dialog box to change the functionality of each mouse button. This is especially useful if you are left-handed and would like to switch the functionality of the left and right mouse button.

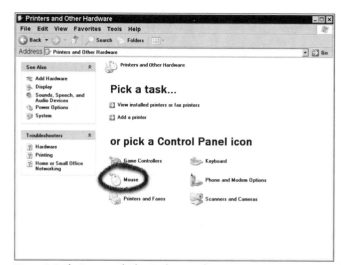

Figure 3-3: The Printers and Other Hardware window

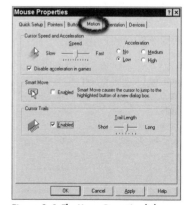

Figure 3-4: The Mouse Properties dialog box, Motion tab

Set Up Your Keyboard

1. Choose Start⇨Control Panel⇨Printers and Other Hardware. In the resulting Printers and Other Hardware window, click the Keyboard link.

2. In the resulting Keyboard Properties dialog box, click the Speed tab (see Figure 3-5) and drag the sliders to adjust the two Character Repeat settings, which do the following:

   • **Repeat Delay:** Affects the amount of time it takes before a typed character is typed again when you hold down a key

   • **Repeat Rate:** Adjusts how quickly a character repeats when you hold down a key after the first repeat character appears

3. Drag the slider to adjust the Cursor Blink Rate. This affects cursors, such as the insertion line that appears in text.

4. Click OK to save and apply changes and close the dialog box.

 If you want to see how the Character Repeat rate settings work in action, click in the box below the two settings and hold down a key to see a demonstration.

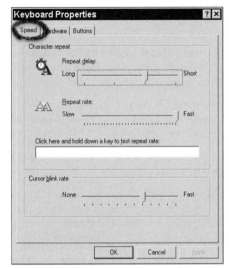

Figure 3-5: The Keyboard Properties dialog box, Speed tab

 If you have trouble with motion, for example, because of arthritis or carpal tunnel syndrome, you may find these settings make it easier for you to get your work done. For example if you can't pick your finger up quickly from a key, a slower repeat rate might save you from typing more instances of a character than you'd intended.

Configure Game Controllers

1. Choose Start➪Control Panel➪Printers and Other Hardware.

2. In the resulting Printers and Other Hardware window, click the Game Controllers link. The Game Controllers dialog box, as shown in Figure 3-6, appears.

3. Click the device you want to configure and then click Properties.

4. On the Test tab of the resulting Properties dialog box, as shown in Figure 3-7, move your controller's buttons. The responses in the corresponding areas should match. For example, if you move up the X Axis button on your controller, the + symbol on the X Axis field should move up.

5. If any settings seem inappropriate, you can click the Settings tab and use the Calibrate feature to recalibrate the controller.

6. When you're done testing, click OK to close the dialog box.

 If you're not sure about how to modify your device settings, try the Reset to Default button on the Settings tab of the Game Controller Properties dialog box. This resets your device to its factory settings, which in most cases are the most appropriate settings to use.

 Calibrating a game controller helps you to make sure that buttons and features are working right. For example, when you recalibrate you can fine-tune functions such as the sensitivity of your controller to movement and the distance you move a joystick before an action registers.

Figure 3-6: The Game Controllers dialog box

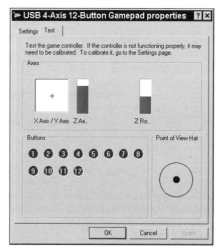

Figure 3-7: The Game Controllers Properties dialog box, Test tab

Setting Up Accessibility Features

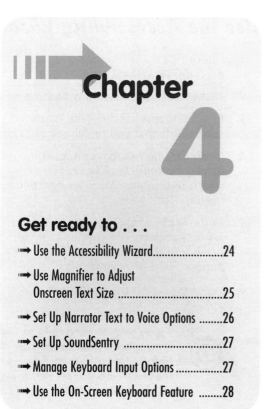

Chapter

4

S ometimes you have to tell Windows XP how to provide access to your hardware features. For example, it doesn't know right off the bat that somebody using a computer has a vision challenge that requires special display settings for a monitor, or that a user prefers a certain mouse cursor, or whether the person in front of the keyboard has a sprained wrist and requires settings that make typing easier.

Windows XP depends on you to make settings that customize its accessibility behavior. This is good news for you because the ability to customize Windows XP gives you a lot of flexibility in how you interact with it.

Here's what you can do to customize Windows XP accessibility options:

➡ Use the Accessibility Wizard to guide you in setting up your system to deal with a variety of input options to help you deal with disability challenges.

➡ Control features that help visually or hearing-challenged users to use a computer, such as text size and audible alerts.

➡ Make settings for your regular and onscreen keyboard.

Get ready to . . .

Use the Accessibility Wizard

1. Choose Start⇨All Programs⇨Accessories⇨Accessibility⇨ Accessibility Wizard.

2. In the resulting Accessibility Options window, click Next.

3. In the text size window (see Figure 4-1), click the text size sample that you prefer and then click Next.

4. In the Display Settings window that opens, select the display options check boxes you prefer for font size, screen resolution, Magnifier, and personalized menu display. Click Next.

5. In the Set Wizard Options window (see Figure 4-2), select the appropriate options for your accessibility needs and then click Next. Follow the screens that appear based on your choices.

6. When you reach the final wizard screen, click Finish to apply your choices.

 If several people use your computer, you might want to set administrator options in the third wizard screen. This allows you to tell Windows XP to turn off options that one person might need, but others don't, such as sticky key, filter key, toggle key, and high contrast, if the computer remains inactive for a certain period of time.

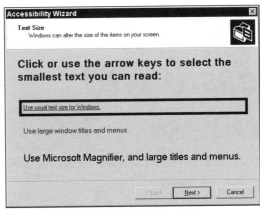

Figure 4-1: The Accessibility Wizard window for text size

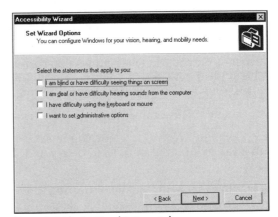

Figure 4-2: The Set Wizard Options window

Use Magnifier to Adjust Onscreen Text Size

1. Choose Start➪All Programs➪Accessories➪Accessibility➪ Magnifier. Click OK in the Magnifier dialog box to proceed.

2. In the Magnifier Settings dialog box shown in Figure 4-3, adjust the settings to your liking:

   • **Magnification Level:** This controls how big things get onscreen.

   • **Tracking:** These settings control what is tracked onscreen, such as your mouse cursor or where your insertion point is for text editing.

   • **Presentation:** Here's where you make settings that affect *inverted colors* (white text on a black background) as well as how and when Magnifier is displayed.

4. Click the Minimize button on the Magnifier Settings dialog box to hide it. (Don't click Exit, or Magnifier turns off.)

5. In the Magnifier window, as shown in Figure 4-4, start working on your computer. If you have the Follow Mouse Cursor option selected in the Magnifier Settings dialog box, you have two cursors onscreen. One cursor appears in the Magnifier window, and one appears in whatever is showing on your computer (for example, your desktop or an open application).

6. Maneuver either cursor to work in your document. (They're both active: It does take some getting used to.)

7. To close the Magnifier window, maximize the Magnifier Settings dialog box by clicking it on the taskbar; then click the Exit or the Close button. Alternately you can right-click the Magnifier window and choose Exit.

Figure 4-3: The Magnifier Settings dialog box

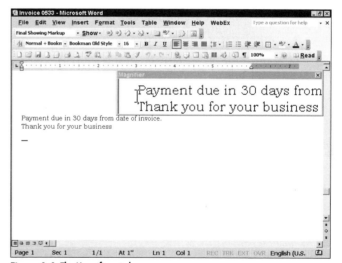

Figure 4-4: The Magnifier window

Set Up Narrator Text to Voice Options

1. Choose Start⇨All Programs⇨Accessories⇨Accessibility⇨ Narrator.

2. A dialog box appears, explaining the function and limitations of Narrator. Click OK to close it.

3. In the resulting Narrator dialog box, select any of the following check boxes (as shown in Figure 4-5):

   - Announce Events on Screen

   - Read Typed Characters

   - Move Mouse Pointer to the Active Item

   - Start Narrator Minimized

4. To control the characteristics of the Narrator voice, click the Voice button.

5. In the resulting Voice Settings dialog box (see Figure 4-6), make changes to the included Microsoft Sam narrator's voice, including changing the Speed, Volume, and Pitch. Click OK to save Voice settings.

6. Click the Minimize button on the Narrator dialog box to hide it, and then begin working on your computer. (*Note:* Narrator can read only in English!)

7. When you finish, display the Narrator dialog box and click the Exit or the Close button.

 By using settings in the Narrator dialog box, you can have Narrator narrate onscreen events or read the text you type. You can also make a setting to have the mouse cursor move to the place onscreen where an action is occurring.

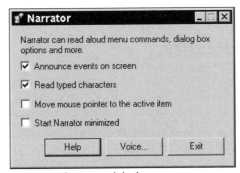

Figure 4-5: The Narrator dialog box

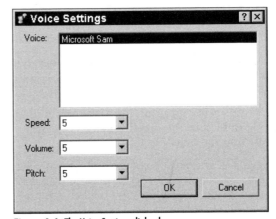

Figure 4-6: The Voice Settings dialog box

Set Up SoundSentry

1. Choose Start⇨Control Panel⇨Accessibility Options. In the Accessibility Options window click Accessibility Options.

2. In the resulting Accessibility Options dialog box, click the Sound tab (see Figure 4-7).

3. Mark the Use SoundSentry check box and click OK to turn on the feature.

 When you choose to have SoundSentry flash a visual warning onscreen whenever a system sound occurs, you can also choose what that visual signal will be. In the Choose the Visual Warning drop-down box on the Sound tab, choose settings for flashing the active caption bar, active window, or desktop.

Manage Keyboard Input Options

1. Choose Start⇨Control Panel⇨Printers and Other Hardware and then click the Keyboard link.

2. In the resulting Keyboard Properties dialog box (see Figure 4-8), click the Repeat Delay slider and drag it to the left to make the delay shorter or to the right to make the delay longer.

3. Click the Repeat Rate slider and drag it to the left to make the rate slower or to the right to make it faster.

4. Click OK to apply the changes.

 If you have difficulty working with a keyboard, adjusting the repeat delay changes the amount of time that elapses before a character repeats when you hold down that key. Changing the repeat rate adjusts the speed at which the character repeats. If you cannot quickly remove your finger from a key, this might help you avoid errors as you type.

Figure 4-7: The Sound tab of the Accessibility Options dialog box

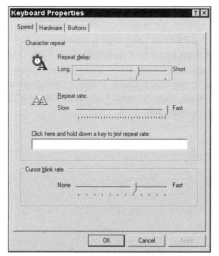

Figure 4-8: The Keyboard Properties dialog box

Use the On-Screen Keyboard Feature

1. Choose Start➪All Programs➪Accessories➪Accessibility➪ On-Screen Keyboard.

2. In the resulting dialog box (see Figure 4-9), click OK.

3. Open a document in any application where you can enter text, and then click the keys on the onscreen keyboard to make entries.

 To use keystroke combinations (such as Ctrl+Z), click the first key (in this case, Ctrl) and then the second key (Z). You don't have to hold down the first key as you do with a regular keyboard.

4. To change settings, such as how you select keys (Typing Mode) or the font used to label keys (Font), choose Settings and then choose one of the four options shown in Figure 4-10.

5. Click the Close button to stop using the onscreen keyboard.

 You can set up the Hover typing mode to activate a key after you hover your mouse over it for a predefined period of time (x number of seconds). If you have arthritis or some other condition that makes clicking your mouse difficult, this option can help you enter text in documents. Choose Settings➪Typing Mode➪Hover to Select to activate the Hover mode.

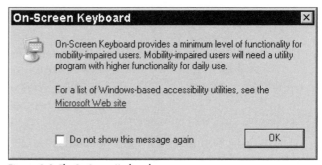

Figure 4-9: The On-Screen Keyboard

Figure 4-10: The Settings menu

Working with Printers, Faxes, and Scanners

A computer is a great storehouse for data, images, and other digital information, but you have to have ways to get things into and out of it. Here are a few key ways to do just that:

➡ Printers allow you to create hard copies of your files on paper, transparencies, or whatever stock your printer can accommodate. To use a printer, you have to have software installed — a *print driver* — and make certain settings to tell your computer how to find the printer.

➡ Faxes let you send an electronic version of documents over your phone line, broadband, or wireless connection. The image received on the other end is an electronic version. Or, you can make settings to have your computer print the transmission to paper via a special fax program.

➡ You use a scanner to create electronic files — pictures, essentially — from hard copies of documents, pictures, or whatever will fit into/ onto your scanner. You can then work with the files, fax or e-mail them, or print them.

Get ready to . . .

Install a Printer

1. Read the instructions that came with the printer. Some printers require that you install software before connecting them, but others can be connected right away.

2. Turn on your computer and then follow the option that fits your needs:

   • If your printer is a Plug and Play device (which most recent printers are), connect it; Windows XP installs what it needs automatically and that's all you need to do.

   • If the device doesn't install automatically, insert the disc that came with the device, follow the onscreen instructions, and you're done!

   • If you don't have a CD or it doesn't automatically walk you through installation, choose Start⇨ Control Panel⇨Printers and Other Hardware⇨ Add A Printer. Proceed to the next step in this list.

3. In the Add Printer Wizard, click Next and then select the Local Printer option (see Figure 5-1). Make sure that the Automatically Detect and Install My Plug and Play Printer check box is selected, and then click Next.

4. In the resulting Local or Network Printer dialog box, you see that Windows XP can't detect any printers. (This is likely; if Windows XP could have, it should have done so automatically — but it doesn't hurt to try, does it?) Click Next.

5. In the resulting Select a Printer Port screen (see Figure 5-2), scroll through the list and select another option if you don't want to use the default LPT1 port. (A *printer port* is essentially where you plug the printer into your computer.) LPT2 and LPT3 are other printer port options, or you might be using a Universal Serial Bus (USB) or network port that should appear in this list. Select the appropriate printer port and click Next.

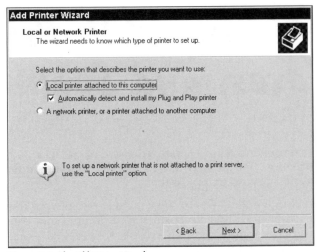

Figure 5-1: The Add Printer Wizard

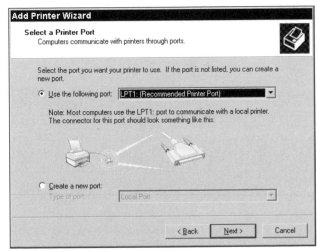

Figure 5-2: The Select a Printer Port dialog box

6. In the resulting Install Printer Software dialog box (see Figure 5-3), choose a manufacturer and then choose a printer. You then have two options:

   • If you have the manufacturer's disc/k, insert it in the appropriate drive and click the Have Disk button. Then click Next.

   • If you don't have the manufacturer's disc/k, click the Windows Update button to see a list of printer drivers; find yours and download it from the Microsoft Web site. Click Next.

7. In the resulting Name Your Printer dialog box, enter a printer name and select Yes or No to determine whether you want this as your *default printer* (the one that Windows XP uses automatically for print jobs). Click Next.

8. In the resulting Print Test Page dialog box, leave the default option of Yes selected. Click Next to print a test page. Click Finish in the Completing the Add Printer Wizard window to install the printer.

9. Go to Control Panel, choose Printers and Other Hardware and then click the View Installed Printers or Fax Printers link. In the printer list, as shown in Figure 5-4, the newly installed printer should be listed.

 If your computer is on a network, you get an additional dialog box in the wizard right after you name the printer. Select the Do Not Share This Printer option to stop others from using the printer, or you can select the Share Name option and enter a printer name to share the printer on your network. This means that others can see and select this printer to print to.

 In the list of printers, the Documents column shows the number of documents that have been sent to any printer, waiting in line to be printed.

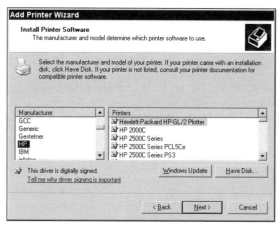

Figure 5-3: The Install Printer Software dialog box

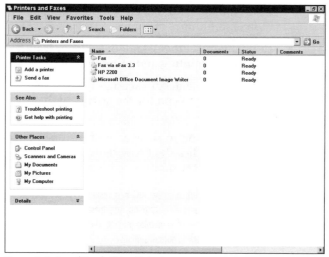

Figure 5-4: Control Panel: All installed printers

Set Printer Preferences

1. Choose Start➪Control Panel➪Printers and Other Hardware➪View Installed Printers or Fax Printers.

2. In the resulting Printers and Faxes window, click a printer in the list and then click the Set Printer Properties link in the Printers Task list to the left.

3. In the Properties dialog box that appears (as shown in Figure 5-5), click the Printing Preferences button on the General tab.

4. In the Printing Preferences dialog box that appears (see Figure 5-6), make any of the following settings:

   • **Quality tab:** Select the default print quality (from draft to best) and default paper type.

   • **Layout tab:** Select the default paper size, paper orientation, and number of copies.

   • **Features tab:** Set the default options for features such as two-sided printing and printing posters.

   • **Color tab:** Make default settings for printing in color or grayscale and for the quality of the color reproduction.

5. Click the OK button to close each of the open dialog boxes, and then click the Close button to close the Printers and Faxes window.

 On the Color tab, note the setting for restoring Factory Settings. If you make changes to the Saturation, Brightness, or Tone settings and they hurt the quality of your color printing, click the Factory Settings button to get back to default settings.

Figure 5-5: A printer's Properties dialog box

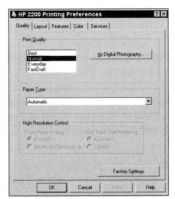 You might have a Services tab in your Printing Preferences dialog box. This is sometimes added for services that your printer manufacturer offers. For example, my computer displays an HP Toolbox button on this tab to calibrate the printer or to print a test page. Also, the settings in the Properties dialog box may differ slightly depending on your printer model; color printers will offer different options from black and white ones, for example.

Figure 5-6: The Printing Preferences dialog box

View Currently Installed Printers

1. Choose Start⇨Control Panel⇨Printers and Other Hardware.

2. In the resulting Printers and Other Hardware window (see Figure 5-7), click the View Installed Printers or Fax Printers link.

3. A list of installed printers appears (see Figure 5-8). You can right-click any printer and then choose Properties to see details about it.

4. Click the Close button to close the window.

 When you click a printer in the list, a list of Printer Tasks appears to the left of the list. You can use links on this list to view current print jobs for that printer, pause printing in progress, or set printer properties. See the preceding task, "Set Printer Preferences," for more about this last procedure.

 Just because you attach a printer to your computer that doesn't mean it's installed. Installing a printer involves installing the printer driver. Most plug and play printers will cause Windows to search for and install a driver when you plug the printer in, but if the driver isn't available, you have to use the New Hardware Wizard to locate and install it. See the next task for more about this.

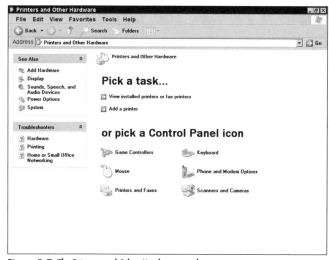

Figure 5-7: The Printers and Other Hardware window

Figure 5-8: The Printers and Faxes window

Make a Printer the Default

1. Choose Start⇨Control Panel⇨Printers and Other Hardware⇨View Installed Printers or Fax Printers.

2. In the resulting Printers and Faxes window (as shown in Figure 5-9), the current default printer is indicated by a small check mark next to it.

3. Right-click any printer that isn't set as the default and choose Set as Default Printer from the shortcut menu, as shown in Figure 5-10.

4. Click the Close button in the Printers and Faxes window to save the new settings.

 To modify printing properties (for example, whether the printer prints in draft or high-quality mode, or uses color or only black-and-white), you can right-click a printer in the Printers and Faxes dialog box and choose Printing Preferences.

 Although all Windows XP programs use the default printer when printing, you can change which printer you print to from within Windows XP applications each time you print. In the Print dialog box in the application is a list of all installed printers, including fax printers. Just choose a different printer for your particular print job and proceed. Your default printer will stay as you set it in the Printers and Faxes window for future print jobs.

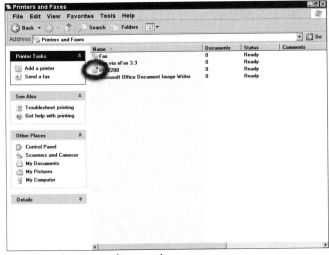

Figure 5-9: The Printers and Faxes window

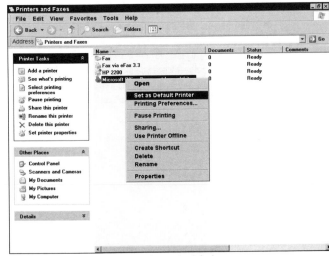

Figure 5-10: The shortcut menu to change the default printer

Remove a Printer

1. Choose Start⇨Control Panel⇨Printers and Other Hardware⇨View Installed Printers or Fax Printers.

2. In the resulting Printers and Faxes window, click a printer in the list to choose it.

3. In the Printer Tasks list that displays to the left, click the Delete This Printer link.

4. In the Printers dialog box that appears (see Figure 5-11), click Yes. Click the Close button to close the Printers and Faxes window.

Rename a Printer

1. Choose Start⇨Control Panel⇨Printers and Other Hardware⇨View Installed Printers or Fax Printers.

2. In the resulting Printers and Faxes window, click a printer in the list to choose it.

3. In the Printer Tasks list that displays to the left, click the Rename This Printer link.

4. In the printer list, the printer name is now available to edit (see Figure 5-12); type a new name and then press Enter to save the new name.

5. Click the Close button to close the Printers and Faxes window.

 Renaming printers can come in handy, especially if you have set up a computer network and various people access differently on it. For example, name your two printers Color Printer in Den and B&W Printer in Basement and there will be no doubt where your document will be printing to!

Figure 5-11: The Printers dialog box confirming the deletion

 If you remove a printer, it is removed from the list of installed printers. You can no longer print to it unless you install it again. See the task, "Install a Printer," if you decide you want to print to that printer again.

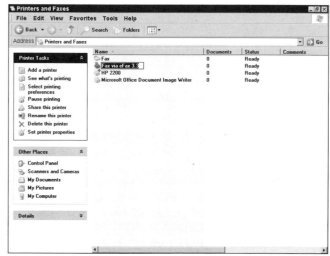

Figure 5-12: A printer in the list ready for renaming

Make Fax Settings

1. Choose Start⇨Control Panel⇨Printers and Other Hardware⇨View Installed Printers or Fax Printers.

2. In the resulting Printers and Faxes window, as shown in Figure 5-13, click a fax in the list and then click the Set Printer Properties link in the Printers Task list to the left.

3. In the Properties dialog box that appears, click the Printing Properties button on the General tab (see Figure 5-14) and make any of the following settings. *Note:* These settings might vary slightly, depending on your fax model.

   - Click the Orientation preview to change orientation between landscape and portrait.

   - Click the arrow for the Paper Size field and either choose another paper size or type paper dimensions in the two fields below.

   - Select the Margins check box to specify whether you want a margin included around the edges of all faxes.

4. Click OK to close the dialog box and then click OK to close the Printers and Faxes window.

You can make other settings for your fax on the various tabs of the Properties dialog box although most of the default settings are usually fine. These include whether to share the fax machine with others, what port it's connected to, the print driver to use for the fax, how documents are *spooled* (queued) to it, and whether colors are controlled automatically or manually. Remember that setting up colors won't have much impact if the recipient of the fax doesn't have a color printer to print your fax with!

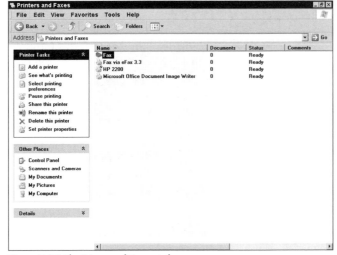

Figure 5-13: The Printers and Faxes window

Remember that a fax is treated like a printer by Windows XP, and you can even follow the procedures given earlier for installing a printer to install your fax machine. You can rename a fax, set fax properties, delete a fax, and so on by following the same procedures outlined in printer tasks earlier in this chapter.

Figure 5-14: The Properties dialog box for a fax

Add a Scanner

1. Connect a scanner to your computer's USB or parallel port, depending on your scanner connection. If your scanner uses Plug and Play technology, Windows XP shows a Found New Hardware message in the Task Bar notification area. Most plug-and-play devices will then automatically install, and that's all you have to do. If that doesn't happen or you are not using a Plug and Play device, click the message.

2. In the resulting Found New Hardware Wizard (this only starts if you don't permit Windows XP to automatically connect to Windows Update) click Yes, This Time Only and then click Next.

3. If you have a CD for the scanner, insert it in your CD drive and click Next. Windows XP searches for your scanner driver software and installs it.

4. Choose Start⇨Control Panel⇨Printers and Other Hardware⇨Scanners and Cameras.

5. In the resulting Scanners and Camera window (see Figure 5-15), click the Add an Imaging Device link in the Imaging Tasks area to the left.

6. In the resulting Scanner and Camera Installation Wizard window, click Next. In the next window (see Figure 5-16), click a Manufacturer in the list on the left and then click a model in the list on the right.

7. Follow the wizard directions based on the model of scanner you choose in Step 6 and whether you have a manufacturer's disc/k or not. When you reach the end of the wizard, click Finish to complete the installation.

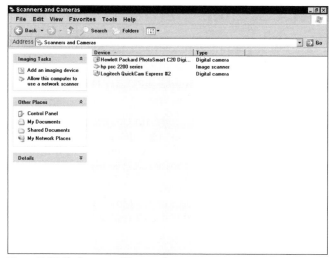

Figure 5-15: The Printers and Faxes window

 If you do not have a disc/k from your manufacturer, you can try to simply use the Windows Scanners and Camera software. Just double-click on the device in the list, and Windows XP will use its own software to run the scanner.

Figure 5-16: The Scanner and Camera Installation Wizard model choices

Check Scanner Settings

1. Choose Start⟹Control Panel⟹Printers and Other Hardware.

2. In the resulting Printers and Other Hardware window, click Scanners and Cameras.

3. In the resulting Scanners and Cameras window, a list of installed scanners appears. Click any scanner in the list and then click the View Device Properties link in the Imaging Tasks area to the left (see Figure 5-17).

4. In the resulting Properties dialog box (see Figure 5-18), review the settings on various tabs. Click the Test Scanner button on the General tab to test the scanner functionality.

5. Click OK to close the Properties dialog box, and then click the Close button to close the Scanners and Camera window.

 The Events tab of the scanner Properties dialog box allows you to make a setting so that Windows XP automatically opens a program when scanning begins. This is handy if you often use one program to work with scanned images, such as a photo imaging or desktop publishing application.

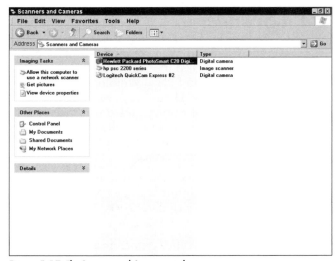

Figure 5-17: The Scanners and Cameras window

Figure 5-18: A scanner's Properties dialog box

Setting Up Your Laptop

Your desktop computer might be all set up and working just the way you want, but your laptop computer is a bit of a different animal. Although most settings work the same, some settings — especially those dealing with battery power — are specific only to laptops.

You might also need to share files between your desktop and laptop computer. That way, when you take your laptop on a trip, you can work on files and then easily update them back at your desk by using the Windows XP Briefcase feature. A briefcase is essentially a shared folder used to exchange and update files.

To work with the laptop that you take on the road, you can do the following:

➡ **Make settings for laptop power management.** Use settings to make choices about how your laptop uses power, set an alarm that warns you when battery power is low, or save battery power by manually putting your laptop into standby mode when not in use.

➡ **Share files between your laptop and PC.** People who use a laptop on the go and a PC at the office need easy ways to share files between the two computers. That's where Windows XP's Briefcase comes in.

Get ready to . . .

Set Up Power Options on Your Laptop

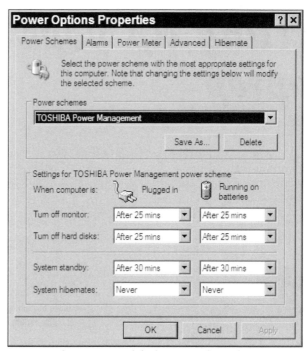

1. Choose Start➪Control Panel➪Performance and Maintenance. On the resulting Performance and Maintenance window, click the Power Options link.

2. On the Power Schemes tab in the resulting Power Options dialog box, as shown in Figure 6-1, click the Power Schemes arrow to display a list of available power schemes, which might include a manufacturer-provided scheme or the Windows XP scheme, for example.

3. Click various fields to make settings for the specified power scheme. Choose from settings that control power for monitor, hard disk, standby, and hibernation for when your laptop is running on battery power or when it's plugged in.

4. Click OK to save new Power Option settings.

 Typically, when your system runs on batteries, you should use shorter periods of time before standby or turning off your monitor kicks in, thereby using less battery power.

 The Hibernate setting, which you enable and disable on the Hibernate tab of the Power Options Properties dialog box, allows you to turn off your computer — but when you turn it on again, you return to wherever you were. So, for example, instead of coming up with the Windows XP desktop, you see the game of Minesweeper that you were playing, all ready to pick up where you left off. This saves battery power and time on trips where work is often interrupted.

Figure 6-1: The Power Options dialog box, Power Scheme tab

Put Your Laptop on Standby Manually

1. Choose Start⇨Turn Off Computer.

2. In the resulting Turn Off Computer dialog box, as shown in Figure 6-2, click Standby.

3. The computer goes into standby mode. To revive it, click your touchpad or mouse, or press Enter on your keyboard.

 Use Standby to save power when you won't use your computer for a short period of time — for example, 10 or 15 minutes — and you don't want to have to spend time powering up Windows XP and opening all the programs and documents you are working with all over again. **Note:** Even in Standby, your battery is slowly drained.

 On the Advanced tab of the Power Options dialog box, you can choose a setting to have your computer go on standby when you press the power button on your computer. If you make this setting, you can come out of standby by pressing the power button (briefly!) again.

 To put your computer into Hibernation instead of Standby, click Ctrl+Standby. Standby is a low power setting, while Hibernation stores whatever is in your hard disk's memory and then shuts down. When you start up again you return to the previous state.

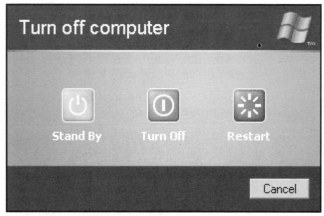

Figure 6-2: The Turn Off Computer dialog box

Set a Low Battery Alarm

1. Choose Start⇨Control Panel⇨Performance and Maintenance. On the resulting Performance and Maintenance window, click the Power Options link.

2. In the resulting Power Options dialog box, click the Alarm tab, as shown in Figure 6-3.

3. Click and drag the Low Battery Alarm slider and the Critical Battery Alarm slider to change the power level at which each alarm sounds.

4. Click the Alarm Action button for either alarm. In the resulting Alarm Action dialog box (see Figure 6-4), enable one or more Notification methods; you can choose either to sound an alarm, display a warning message, or both.

5. Select the When the Alarm Goes Off, the Computer Will check box. Then click the Alarm Action arrow and choose an action for the computer to perform when the alarm sounds.

6. Click OK twice to save the settings and close both dialog boxes.

 Your computer manufacturer might have installed a power management interface that provides special features for your model. In some cases, the manufacturer sets things so that you can't access Windows XP's power management features at all but have to use those from the manufacturer. However, in most cases, the settings offered are very similar to those you find in Windows XP.

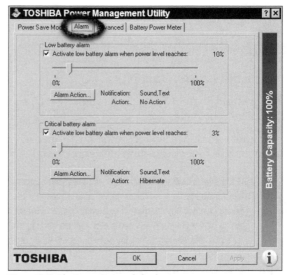

Figure 6-3: The Power Options dialog box

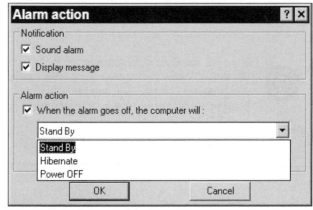

Figure 6-4: The Alarm Action dialog box

Create a Briefcase

1. Choose Start⇨My Computer.

2. In the resulting My Computer window, double-click your hard drive letter (usually C).

3. Choose File⇨New⇨Briefcase (see Figure 6-5). A new briefcase folder is created.

4. Right-click the folder and choose Rename. The folder name opens for editing (see Figure 6-6). Type a new name.

 You can also create a briefcase on your desktop for easier access. Right-click the desktop and choose New⇨Briefcase. The New Briefcase item appears. If you create a lot of briefcases, consider renaming this one to reflect the type of information you will share there (see Step 4 above).

 If you're looking for the original document (the counterpart to the copy of the document in the briefcase), you can use this method to locate it: Choose Update Status, and then click Find Original.

 If a file in your briefcase shows its status as 'orphan', that means the file in the briefcase is not synchronized with any other file; in other words, the connection that causes each file to update according to changes in the other has been severed. This is done using the Split from Original command on the Briefcase menu. The easiest fix is to just copy the original over into the briefcase again.

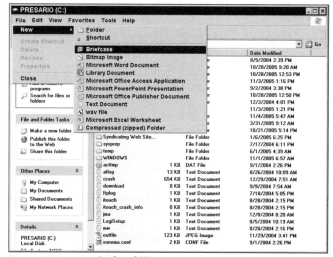

Figure 6-5: Creating a briefcase folder

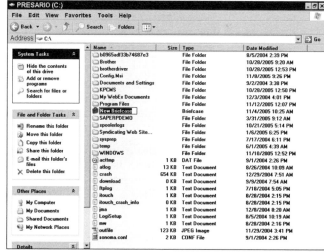

Figure 6-6: Renaming a Briefcase

Synchronize Files by Using Briefcase Over a Network

1. If sharing files from a briefcase to another computer, connect the two computers, either over a network or with a cable. If sharing files between a computer and removable media such as a CD-ROM, insert the media in the appropriate drive.

2. Locate the folders or files you want to share on a hard drive or removable media via Windows Explorer, and then click and drag them into the briefcase. You might need to reduce the size of the My Computer and other Windows Explorer windows so you can view them side-by-side onscreen. The files are now available to both locations via the shared briefcase folder.

3. Disconnect the computers or remove the media and go about your business, working on documents away from your PC. When you return, connect the computers again or reinsert the removable media in a drive, and back on the original computer where you shared the files, double-click the briefcase to open it. Choose Briefcase↪ Update All (see Figure 6-7).

4. The Update Briefcase dialog box appears (see Figure 6-8). To change an action, right-click the item and choose a different action. For example, if the action is Delete, you can choose Don't Delete for that item.

5. Click on items in the briefcase and click the Update button to update the documents in the briefcase on the host computer. Both computers now have access to the latest versions of the files.

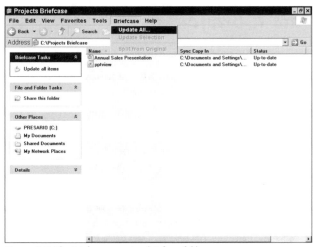

Figure 6-7: The Briefcase menu in a briefcase folder

Although the Shared Documents folder on a network allows networked computers to access the same files, Briefcase comes in handy if you take one computer off the network, work on files, and then return to the network and want to update the files that reside there. You could also create a briefcase on a removable disc (such as a CD-ROM), make changes on another computer, copy the briefcase back onto the network or standalone computer, and then perform an update.

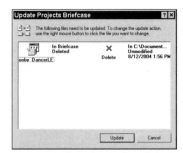

Figure 6-8: The Update Briefcase dialog box

Part II
The Brains of the Beast

The 5th Wave   By Rich Tennant

Before installing Windows XP, Dwayne prepares to partition the hard drive.

RICHTENNANT

Working with Windows XP

*Y*ou might think of Windows XP as a set of useful accessories, such as games, a calculator, and a paint program for playing around with images, but Windows XP is first and foremost an operating system. Windows XP's main purpose is to enable you to run and manage other software applications, from programs that manage your finances to the latest 3-D computer action game. By using the best methods for accessing and running software with Windows XP, you save time; setting up Windows XP in the way that works best for you can make your life easier.

In this chapter, you explore several simple and very handy techniques for launching and navigating between applications. You go through step-by-step procedures ranging from opening an application to resizing application windows, and from logging on to Windows XP to emptying the Recycle Bin. Along the way, you discover the Windows XP Start Menu (a Command Central for running programs) and the Quick Launch Bar. (This might sound like a salad bar at a fast food restaurant, but it's actually the area of the Windows XP taskbar that lets you open frequently used programs.)

Here, then, are the procedures that you can use to launch, navigate, and organize programs in Windows XP (note that other versions of Windows might work differently).

Get ready to . . .

Log On and Off Windows XP

1. Turn on your computer to begin the Windows XP start-up sequence.

2. In the resulting Windows XP Welcome screen, enter your password and click the green arrow button. Windows XP verifies your password and displays the Windows XP desktop as shown in Figure 7-1. (**Note:** If you haven't set up the password protection feature or more than one user, you're taken directly to the Windows XP desktop.)

3. To log off the current user, first save any open documents and close any open applications and then choose Start➪ Log Off. Windows XP logs off and displays a list of users. To log on again, click a user icon.

 To create another user choose Start➪Control Panel➪User Accounts, and then click Create a New Account. Follow instructions to enter a name for the account and set a password for it, if you like.

 To log on as another user (for example, if somebody else in your family is logged on and you want to change to your user account), choose Start➪Log Off and then click the Switch User button. Click your user name in the list of users that appears (the same list that you see on the Windows XP Welcome screen) and then follow the steps in this task to finish logging on. Note that for this to work you have to enable Fast User Switching in the User Account settings.

Figure 7-1: The Windows XP desktop

 Once you have set up more than one user, before you get to the password screen you have to click on the icon for the user you wish to log on as.

Open an Application

1. Launch an application by using any of the following three methods:

   - Choose Start⇨All Programs. Locate the program name on the All Programs menu and click it; if clicking it displays a submenu, click the program item on that menu (as shown in Figure 7-2).

   - Double-click a program shortcut icon on the desktop (see Figure 7-3).

   - The taskbar should be displayed by default, but if it's not, press the Windows key (on your keyboard) to display it, and then click an icon on the Quick Launch Bar, just to the right of the Start button. Note that the Quick Launch Bar is not displayed by default. See the task Work with the Quick Launch Bar for more about this.

2. When the application opens, if it's a game, play it; if it's a spreadsheet, enter numbers into it; if it's your e-mail program, start deleting junk mail. . . . You get the idea.

Not every program that's installed on your computer appears as a desktop shortcut or Quick Launch Bar icon. To add a program to the Quick Launch Bar, see the task "Work with the Quick Launch Bar," later in this chapter. To add a desktop shortcut, see Chapter 2.

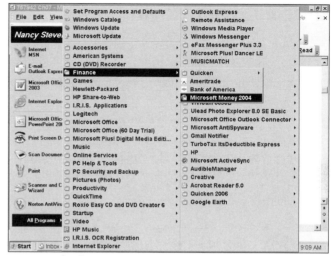

Figure 7-2: The All Programs menu

Figure 7-3: Desktop shortcuts and the taskbar

Close an Application

1. With an application open, first save any open documents and then close them by using one of these methods:

   • Click the Close button in the upper-right corner of the window.

   • Choose File⇨Exit (see Figure 7-4).

2. The application closes. If you haven't saved any documents before trying to close the application, you see a dialog box asking whether you want to save the document (see Figure 7-5). Click Yes or No, depending on whether you want to save your changes.

 To save a document choose File⇨Save and use settings in the Save dialog box that appears to name the file and specify which folder to save it to.

 Note that choosing File⇨Exit closes all open documents in an application. Choose File⇨Close to close only the currently active document and keep the application and any other open documents open.

 You don't have to close an application to open or switch to another. To switch between open applications click Alt+Tab on your keyboard and use the arrow keys to move to the application (or document if multiple documents are open in an application) in which you want to work.

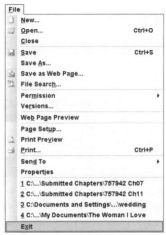

Figure 7-4: Choosing the Exit command

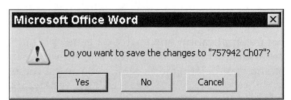

Figure 7-5: Saving changes to open documents

Resize Application Windows

1. With an application open and maximized, click the Restore Down button (showing two overlapping windows) in the top-right corner of the program window. The window reduces in size.

2. To enlarge a window that has been restored down to again fill the screen, click the Maximize button (see Figure 7-6). (*Note:* This is in the same place as the Restore Down button; this button toggles as one or the other, depending on whether you have the screen reduced in size or maximized. A ScreenTip identifies the button when you pass your mouse over it.)

 With a window maximized, you can't move the window around on the desktop. If you reduce a window in size, you can then click and hold the title bar to drag the window around on the desktop, which is one way to view more than one window on your screen at the same time. You can also click and drag the corners of the window to resize it to any size you want.

Switch between Application Windows

1. Open two or more programs. The last program that you open is the active program.

2. Press and hold Alt+Tab to open a small box, as shown in Figure 7-7, revealing all opened programs.

3. Release the Tab key but keep Alt held down. Press Tab to cycle through the icons representing open programs.

4. Release the Alt key, and Windows XP switches to whichever program is selected. To switch back to the last program that was active, simply press Alt+Tab, and that program becomes the active program once again.

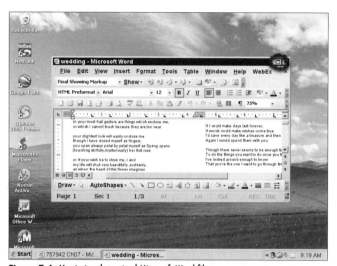

Figure 7-6: Maximize the resized Microsoft Word file

 All open programs also appear as items on the Windows XP taskbar. You can click any running program on the taskbar to make it the active program. If the taskbar isn't visible, press the Windows key on your keyboard to display it.

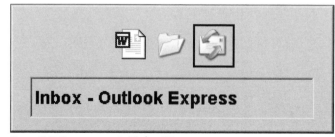

Figure 7-7: Open programs in Windows XP

Create a Desktop Shortcut

1. Choose Start⇨All Programs and locate the program on the list of programs that appears.

2. Right-click an item and choose Send To⇨Desktop (create shortcut) (see Figure 7-8).

3. The shortcut appears on the desktop (see Figure 7-9). Double-click the icon to open the application.

 Occasionally, Windows XP offers to delete desktop icons that you haven't used in a long time. Let it. The desktop should be reserved for frequently-used programs, files, and folders. You can always re-create shortcuts easily if you need them again.

 To clean up your desktop manually, right-click the desktop and choose Properties. On the Desktop tab, click the Customize Desktop button. In the Desktop Items dialog box that appears, click the Clean Desktop Now button, which runs the Clean Desktop Wizard. This offers you options for removing little-used shortcuts.

 If you're working on a project, consider creating a shortcut to that project folder. Or, if you're figuring out your way around Windows XP for the first time, consider creating a shortcut to the Help and Support Center.

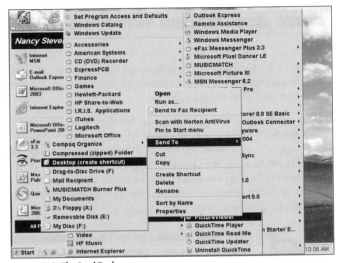

Figure 7-8: The Send To shortcut menu

Figure 7-9: A shortcut on the desktop

Arrange Icons on the Desktop

1. Right-click the Windows XP desktop and in the resulting shortcut menu, as shown in Figure 7-10, choose Arrange Icons By and then choose Type. Make sure that Auto Arrange isn't selected. (If it is selected, deselect it before choosing Type.)

2. Click any icon and drag it to another location on the desktop — for example, to separate it from other desktop icons so you can find it easily (see Figure 7-11).

 If you've rearranged your desktop by moving items hither, thither, and yon, and you want your icons into orderly rows along the left side of your desktop, snap them into place with the Auto Arrange feature. Right-click the desktop and then choose Arrange By⇨Auto Arrange.

 Want to quickly hide all your desktop icons? Say the boss is headed your way and all you've got there is games? Right-click the desktop and choose Arrange Icons By⇨Show Desktop Icons. Poof! They're all gone, and your job is secure. Just repeat the process to display them again.

 Want help organizing your desktop? Click on the desktop and choose Arrange Items by⇨Run Desktop Cleanup Wizard. The wizard provides a list of desktop shortcuts and lets you click checkboxes to select and deselect which shortcuts to include from a single dialog box.

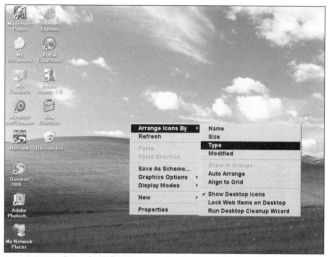

Figure 7-10: The Desktop shortcut menu

Figure 7-11: A shortcut moved to one side of the desktop

Work with the Quick Launch Bar

1. Locate the Quick Launch Bar on the taskbar just to the right of the Start button; if it's not visible, right-click the taskbar and choose Toolbars⇨Quick Launch from the shortcut menu (see Figure 7-12). By default, it includes the Show Desktop icon and some Microsoft programs, such as Internet Explorer and Outlook.

2. To place any application on the Quick Launch Bar, as shown in Figure 7-13, click that application's icon (or shortcut) on the Windows XP desktop and drag it to the Quick Launch Bar. (If you want help creating a desktop shortcut, see the task, "Create a Desktop Shortcut" earlier in this chapter.)

Figure 7-12: The Toolbars menu

 If you have more programs in this area than can be shown on the taskbar, click the arrows to the right of the Quick Launch Bar; a shortcut menu of programs appears. However, don't clutter up your Quick Launch Bar, which can make it unwieldy. Logical candidates to place here are your Internet browser, your e-mail program, and programs that you use every day, such as a word processor or calendar program.

Figure 7-13: Icons on the Quick Launch bar

 When the Quick Launch Bar is displayed, the Show Desktop button is available. When you click this button, all open applications are reduced to taskbar icons. It's a quick way to clean your desktop or hide what you're up to!

Customize the Start Menu

1. Press the Windows key on your keyboard to display the Start menu. Right-click anywhere on an empty part of the Start menu and choose Properties.

2. In the resulting Taskbar and Start Menu Properties dialog box, click the Customize button to display the Customize Start Menu dialog box, as shown in Figure 7-14. You can do the following:

- Click to set standard or large icon size.

- Click the up or down arrows on the Number of Programs on Start Menu text box to display more or fewer of your frequently-used programs.

- Use the lists of alternate Internet and e-mail programs to select different applications to appear on the Start menu.

3. Click the Advanced tab to display it. Determine what items you want to display on the Start menu and select or deselect items in the Start Menu Items list.

4. After you finish making selections, click OK to save the new settings. Your Start menu reflects your changes, showing items for accessing and running programs and features, such as the ones in Figure 7-15.

 Right-click the list of programs in the Start menu and choose Sort By Name to alphabetize the list. Folders get reordered to appear first, followed by individual programs.

Figure 7-14: The Customize Start Menu dialog box

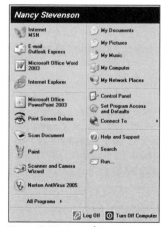

Figure 7-15: A typical Start menu, customized for the programs most used

Start an Application Automatically

1. Right-click the Start menu button and choose Explore, as shown in Figure 7-16.

2. In the resulting Windows XP Explorer dialog box is a list of folders on the left side. Click the plus sign next to the Start Menu folder, then the Programs folder, and then the Startup folder to see a list of programs in it.

3. Click a program from the list and drag it into the Startup folder (see Figure 7-17).

4. When you finish moving programs into the Startup folder, click the Close button in the upper-right corner. The programs you moved will now open every time Windows XP is started.

 If you place too many programs in Startup, it may take a minute or two before you can get to work, while you wait for programs to load. Don't overfill your Startup folder: Use it just for the programs you need most often.

 You can remove an application from the right side of the Start menu by right-clicking the Start button and choosing Properties from the contextual menu that appears. On the Start Menu tab, click the Customize button. In the Customize dialog box, click the Advanced tab and then clear the check box for the item you want to remove.

Figure 7-16: Opening Windows XP Explorer

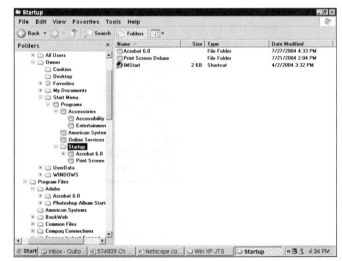

Figure 7-17: The Startup folder contents

Set Program Access Defaults

1. Choose Start➪Control Panel➪Add or Remove Programs.

2. In the resulting Add or Remove Programs window, as shown in Figure 7-18, click the arrow next to any of the choices to see specifics about the programs that they set as defaults.

3. Select one of the following options to see detailed information (see Figure 7-19):

   • **Computer Manufacturer:** Restores the defaults set when your computer shipped. Your version of Windows XP might/might not have been set up with this option by your computer manufacturer.

   • **Microsoft Windows:** Sets defaults used by Windows XP.

   • **Non-Microsoft:** Removes access to Microsoft programs and uses currently set-up programs as defaults. This is popular with Linux users and Microsoft haters.

   • **Custom:** Allows you to set up the programs that you have currently set as default, Microsoft programs, or a combination.

4. Click OK to save your settings.

 When you turn off the Enable Access to this Program option by removing the check mark in the Custom option, you don't find it on the Start menu any longer. It's still on your hard drive, though, and you can open it by using Windows XP Explorer.

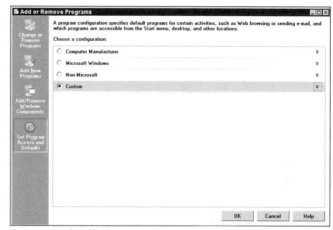

Figure 7-18: The Add or Remove Programs window

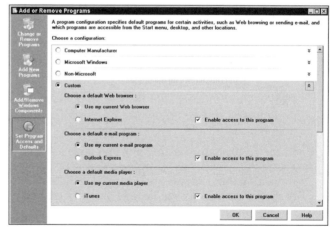

Figure 7-19: Various custom access options

Set the Date and Time

1. Press the Windows key on your keyboard to display the taskbar if it isn't visible.

2. Right-click the Date/Time item on the far right of the taskbar and choose Adjust Date/Time from the shortcut menu that appears.

3. In the Date and Time Properties dialog box that appears (see Figure 7-20), click a different date in the displayed month to change the date. Click the spinner arrows on the time setting to change the time.

4. Click OK to apply the new settings and close the dialog box.

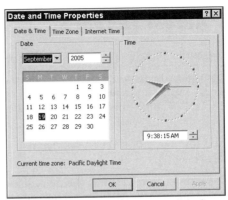

Figure 7-20: The Date and Time Properties dialog box

 If the month or year for which you want to set the date to aren't displayed when you open the Date and Time Properties dialog box, choose a different month from the month drop-down list or use the spinner arrows to move to a different year.

Empty the Recycle Bin

1. Right-click the Recycle Bin icon on the Windows XP desktop and choose Empty Recycle Bin from the menu that appears.

2. In the confirmation dialog box that appears (see Figure 7-21), click Yes. A progress dialog box appears indicating the contents are being deleted. Remember that after you empty the Recycle Bin, all files in it are unavailable to you.

Figure 7-21: Confirming the Empty Recycle Bin command.

 Up until the moment you permanently delete items by performing the preceding steps, you can retrieve items in the Recycle Bin by right-clicking the desktop icon and choosing Open. Select the item you want to retrieve and then click the Restore This Item link on the left side of the Recycle Bin window.

Shut Down Your Computer

1. Choose Start⇨Turn Off Computer.

2. In the resulting Turn Off Computer dialog box shown in Figure 7-22, click the Turn Off button to shut the computer down completely; if you want to *reboot* (turn off and turn back on) your computer, click the Restart button.

 If you're going away for a while but don't want to have to go through the whole booting up sequence complete with Windows XP music when you return, you don't have to turn off your computer. Just click the Stand By button in Step 2 to put your computer into a kind of sleeping state where the screen goes black and the fan shuts down. When you get back, click your mouse button or press Enter, your computer springs to life, and whatever programs and documents you had open are still open.

 If your computer freezes up for some reason, you can turn it off in a couple of ways. Click Ctrl+Alt+Delete twice in a row, or press the power button on your CPU and hold it until the computer shuts down.

Figure 7-22: The Turn Off Computer dialog box

 Don't simply turn off your computer at the power source unless you have to because of a computer crash. Windows may not start up properly the next time you turn it on if you don't follow the proper shut down procedure.

Managing Memory

Your brain cells offer a certain amount of storage space for memories, which can range from your phone number to the name of your high school prom date. But after your brain fills up, it might dump a few out-of-date memories in order to store others (goodbye, prom date; hello, your baby's first steps).

Your computer acts in a similar way: It contains a certain amount of capacity to store data. After that capacity *(memory)* is filled up, your PC needs your help to clean it out or add more memory. When your computer is low on memory, you might find that you can't save any more files to your hard drive. Or your computer might begin to experience performance problems, running slowly or crashing on a regular basis.

To avoid these problems, occasionally check your memory and free up or add memory as needed using Disk Cleanup to get rid of data that is no longer used by any program and Disk Defragmenter to organize data more efficiently on your hard drive. You can add a memory card, organize data more efficiently, and perform maintenance tasks to clean out old data to free up memory for more current information.

Chapter

8

Get ready to . . .

Check Installed Memory

1. Choose Start⇨My Computer.

2. In the resulting My Computer window (see Figure 8-1), click the View System Information link.

3. In the resulting System Properties dialog box, click the General tab to view the total memory, located toward the bottom (see Figure 8-2).

The memory listed in the System Properties dialog box is RAM (random access memory). This is the memory that you install with memory cards, and it is used to temporarily store data while your computer is running programs. The more RAM you have, the better Windows XP will perform.

Memory comes in different varieties. Dual Inline Memory Modules (DIMM) are most common on more recent PCs. Older PCs use Single Inline Memory Modules (SIMM). You have to get the right type of memory for your PC chip. Try a site such as Crucial Technology (www.crucial.com) to help you figure this out.

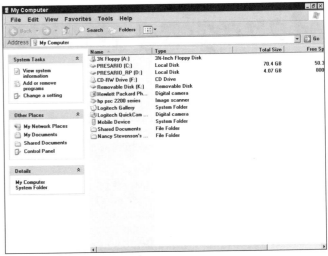

Figure 8-1: The My Computer window

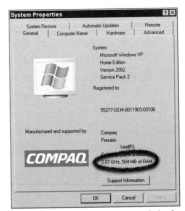

Figure 8-2: The System Properties dialog box

Free Up Memory with Disk Cleanup

1. Choose Start➪All Programs➪Accessories➪System Tools➪ Disk Cleanup, as shown in Figure 8-3.

2. *If you have more than one hard drive:* In the dialog box that appears, select the drive you want to clean from the drop-down list and then click OK. (See Chapter 8 for more about partitioning a hard drive to create multiple hard drives for memory efficiency.) If you have only one hard drive Windows XP automatically starts cleaning up the C: drive.

3. The resulting dialog box tells you that Disk Cleanup is calculating how much space can be cleared on your hard drive. Go ahead and read your daily horoscope while Disk Cleanup does its thing.

4. After a few moments, the Disk Cleanup For *Drive* dialog box, as shown in Figure 8-4, appears. It displays the suggested files to delete in a list. (Those to be deleted have a check mark.) If you want to select additional files in the list to delete, click to place a check mark next to them. If there are some you want to keep, click to uncheck them.

5. After you select all the files to delete, click OK. The selected files are deleted.

 Click the More Options tab in the Disk Cleanup dialog box to look at Windows XP components and program files that you don't use and system restore points that you might delete to save even more space.

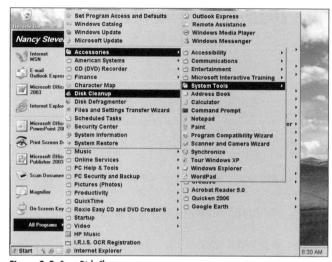

Figure 8-3: Start Disk Cleanup

Figure 8-4: The Disk Cleanup dialog box

Run Disk Defragmenter

1. Choose Start➪All Programs➪Accessories➪System Tools➪ Disk Defragmenter.

2. In the resulting Disk Defragmenter window, as shown in Figure 8-5, select your hard drive (usually the C: drive).

3. To analyze your drive and see what defragmenting will do to it, click the Analyze button. After a few moments, a dialog box appears. Click View Report.

4. An analysis report like the one shown in Figure 8-6 appears. It suggests one of two courses of action:

- **No defragmentation is necessary.** In this case, simply click Close and then close the Disk Defragmenter window.

- **Defragmentation is recommended.** In this case, click the Defragment button. When the Defragmenter is done, close the Disk Defragmenter window.

 Disk defragmenting can take a while. If you have an energy-saving feature enabled, such as a screen saver, it could cause the defragmenter to stop and start all over again. Try doing this overnight, while you're happily dreaming of much more interesting things.

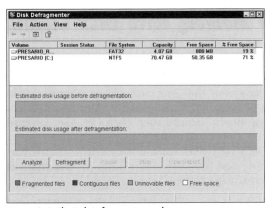

Figure 8-5: The Disk Defragmenter window

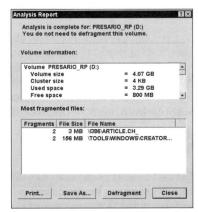

Figure 8-6: The results of a hard drive analysis

Add Memory

1. To install a memory card, turn off your desktop computer and disconnect all power and other cables from it.

2. Open the PC chassis (see Figure 8-7). Check your user's manual for this procedure, which usually involves removing a few screws and popping the cover off your tower.

3. Touch a metal object with your hand to get rid of any static charge before you reach inside the computer.

4. Locate the slots for memory cards. There are typically three or four in a group. Again, check your manual for the exact location in your system.

5. If you are replacing an old memory card with a new one, remove the old card first. If your system has clips at either end of the slot, move them out of the way first. If you are adding an additional memory card, you can simply use an empty slot. See your user's manual to see which slots might makes sense for the size memory card you are inserting.

6. Remove the new memory card from its sealed bag; handling the card by its edges, line it up with the slot and insert it firmly but gently (see Figure 8-8). If your model requires it, snap the clips in place to hold in the card.

7. Make sure that you didn't disconnect any wires or leave any loose screws inside the PC chassis; then replace the computer cover and reinsert the screws.

8. Plug the computer in and turn it on. Your computer should sense the new memory when it starts up.

 Warning: Never force a memory card into a slot. Doing so can damage the card or your PC. If the card won't insert easily, you might be holding it the wrong way. Try reversing it, and insert it again.

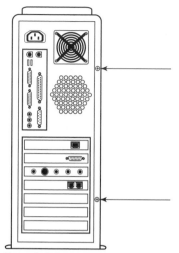

Figure 8-7: Opening your computer

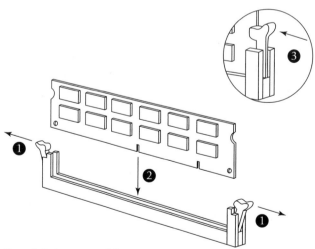

Figure 8-8: A memory card slot

Initialize a New Hard Drive

1. After installing a new hard drive (see your user's manual for instructions, which will vary by system), choose Start⇨Control Panel⇨Administrative Tools.

2. In the resulting Administrative Tools window click Computer Management, and then click Disk Management in the Computer Management window that appears.

3. In the resulting Disk Management window (see Figure 8-9), right-click the new drive and then choose Initialize Disk.

4. In the resulting Initialize Disk dialog box, click OK.

 After you initialize a new hard drive, you should also follow the preceding procedure to partition it (see the following task). The New Partition Wizard you access for that task takes you through both partitioning and formatting the drive. For your hard drive, during that procedure, you should format the drive as the primary partition and use all the space on the drive.

Partition a Disk

1. Choose Start⇨Control Panel⇨Performance and Maintenance⇨Administrative Tools.

2. In the resulting Administrative Tools window, double-click the Computer Management link.

3. In the resulting Computer Management window (as shown in Figure 8-10), choose Disk Management in the left pane, right-click a basic disk in the right pane (this is usually your hard drive) that isn't allocated, and then choose New Partition.

4. Follow the steps in the New Partition Wizard to create the new partition.

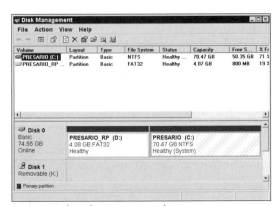

Figure 8-9: The Disk Management window.

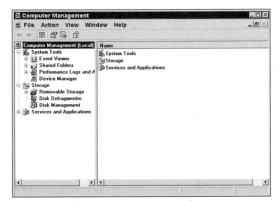

Figure 8-10: The Computer Management window

 A new partition can free up some memory and make your system utilize memory more efficiently. But just so you know, you have to be logged on as a system administrator to complete the steps listed here. If you are an individual desktop user, check settings under User Accounts in the Control Panel to set up administrator status. If you're on a network, ask your network administrator about these rights.

Setting Up Software

Chapter

9

*T*he whole point of that computer sitting on your desk (or floor, or lap) is to run software programs. Software can range from the coolest new game with wow graphics to get-down-to-business spreadsheet or word processing programs. However, all software programs have some things in common.

First, unless a program comes already loaded on your computer, it has to be installed. Conversely, if there is software on your computer you don't need (you know, like that tax program you used in 2000 that's been hanging around for years), you can remove it.

Windows XP is software, too (software that runs your software), and you need to take some special care to keep it current and secure. Microsoft periodically creates updates for Windows XP that you can download from the Internet. Some of these updates fix problems with the software *(bugs)* or add security or other features. You can get these updates online by initiating an update session yourself or by using automatic update features.

Get ready to . . .

Check for Installed Software

1. Choose Start⇨Control Panel⇨Add or Remove Programs.

2. In the resulting Add or Remove Programs window (see Figure 9-1), click the Sort By drop-down list. Click one of the four options to sort the list of programs installed on your computer:

- **Name**

- **Size**

- **Frequency of Use**

- **Date Last Used**

3. Click and drag the scroll bar to view all the installed programs on your computer.

 You won't see any Windows XP components in the Add or Remove Programs window. To view those, you have to click the Add/Remove Windows Components in the bar along the left side of the window. All Windows XP components are listed, along with the space they are taking up on your hard drive.

 If you want to see any updates you have made to installed software, with the Add/Remove Programs window displayed, click the Show Updates checkbox.

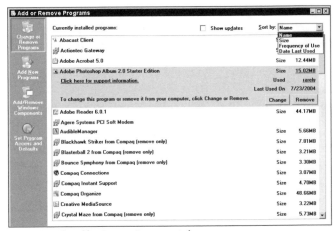

Figure 9-1: The Add or Remove Programs window

 If you're considering uninstalling a program, note that when you click an item in the Add/Remove programs list you see an item that tells you how often you have used the program. If there's something you haven't used for years, that may affect your decision to get rid of it.

Install Software

1. If you insert a software CD and nothing happens, choose Start⇨Control Panel⇨Add or Remove Programs to open the Add or Remove Programs window.

 In many cases, you don't need to go through Windows XP to install software. Just pop the software CD into your CD drive, and the installation process begins. Give Windows XP a vacation — after all, it works hard day after day, right?

2. Click the Add New Programs button on the left, and then click the CD or Floppy button, as shown in Figure 9-2.

3. When the resulting Install Program From Floppy Disk or CD-ROM dialog box appears (see Figure 9-3), click Next to run the software.

4. Follow the prompts for the software installation. (*Note:* Some programs require that you reboot your computer, so you might have to restart your computer to complete the setup of the new program.)

 If you install software and later want to change which features of the program have been installed, go to Control Panel. When you choose Add or Remove Programs, find the software in the list that appears and then click the Change/Remove button.

Figure 9-2: The Add or Remove Programs window

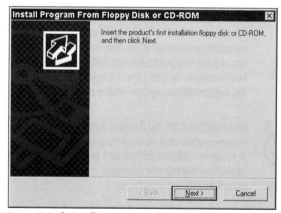

Figure 9-3: The Install Program From Floppy Disk or CD-ROM Wizard

Remove an Application

1. Choose Start⇨Control Panel⇨Add or Remove Programs.

2. In the resulting Add or Remove Programs window, as shown in Figure 9-4, click a program and then click the Change/Remove button. Although some programs will display their own uninstall screen, in most cases, a confirmation dialog box appears (see Figure 9-5).

3. If you're sure that you want to remove the program, click Yes in the confirmation dialog box. A dialog box shows the progress of the procedure; it disappears when the program has been removed.

4. Click the Close button to close the Add or Remove Programs dialog box.

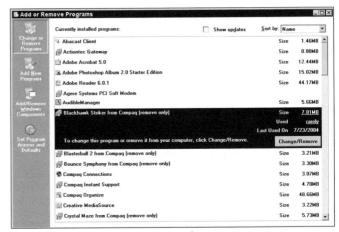

Figure 9-4: The Add or Remove Programs window

With some programs that include multiple applications, such as Microsoft Office, you might want to remove only one program, not the whole shooting match. For example, you might decide that you have no earthly use for Access but can't let a day go by without using Excel and Word — so why not free up some hard drive space and send Access packing? If you want to modify a program in this way, click the Change button in Step 2 of this task rather than the Remove button. The dialog box that appears allows you to select the programs that you want to install or uninstall.

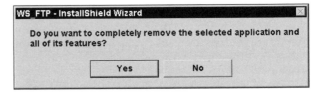

Figure 9-5: The Removal Confirmation dialog box

Warning: If you click the Change or Remove Programs link, there are some programs that will simply be removed with no further input from you. Be really sure that you don't need a program before you remove it, or that you have the original software on disk so you can reinstall it should you need it again.

Add or Remove Windows XP Components

1. Choose Start⇨Control Panel⇨Add or Remove Programs.

2. In the resulting Add or Remove Programs window, click Add/Remove Windows Components.

3. In the Windows Components Wizard window that appears (see Figure 9-6), click in blank check boxes to choose items to install and click in check boxes with a check mark to remove those components.

4. When the final wizard dialog box appears, click Finish.

 Be very careful about removing Windows XP components. Some of them might be needed to efficiently operate your computer system. If you do want to remove a component, consider creating a system restore point before you do (see chapter 22).

 You can click the Details button in the Windows Components Wizard to see more information about programs; for example you may see a larger program broken down into two or more programs, with detail about how much space each will use on your hard drive. You then have the option of installing some, but not all, to save space.

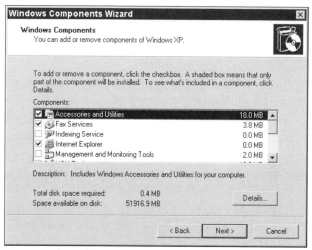

Figure 9-6: The Windows Components Wizard

 If you see a shaded checkbox in the Windows Component Wizard window it means that a portion of the item is available to be installed. For example, if you are not on a network certain networking services won't be available to you.

Run Windows Update

1. Connect to the Internet and then choose Start➪All Programs➪Windows Update.

2. On the resulting Microsoft Update Web page, click the Express Button (shown in Figure 9-7).

3. When the scan is complete, the Pick Updates to Install page appears. Click the Review and Install Updates link.

4. On the resulting Web page (see Figure 9-8), use the scrollbar to review the recommended updates, clicking the Remove button for any that you don't want to install.

5. After you click Install Now, you see the download progress.

 Updates typically include security updates to Microsoft products; updated drivers for peripherals such as printers, mouse, and monitors; and updates to Microsoft products to fix *bugs,* as they're affectionately known among computer geeks. Bugs are bad, but updates are usually good.

 Warning: If you're running Windows XP on a network, your network security settings could stop you from using the Windows Update feature. However, the good news is that if you're on a network, your network administrator should be taking care of the updates for you.

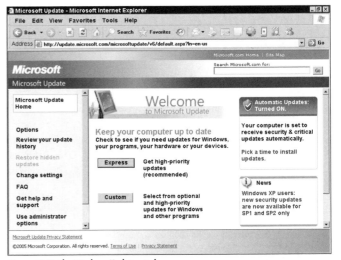

Figure 9-7: The Windows Update window

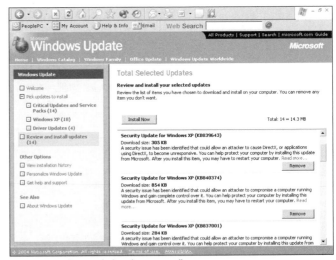

Figure 9-8: Selecting which updates to install

Manage Automatic Updates

1. Choose Start➪Control Panel, click the Performance and Maintenance link, and then click the System link.

2. In the System Properties dialog box, click the Automatic Updates tab to display it (see Figure 9-9).

3. Select one of the four radio buttons to specify how you want to manage updates:

   • **Automatic:** Downloads and installs updates at the specified frequency and time of day you select from the two drop-down boxes here.

   • **Download Updates For Me:** Lets updates be downloaded but not installed until you choose to do so.

   • **Notify Me:** Causes Windows XP to send you a message that downloads are available — but they are not downloaded nor installed.

   • **Turn Off Automatic Updates:** Turns off this feature entirely. To get updates, you have to go to the Windows Update Web site, which you can do by clicking the link provided onscreen.

4. Click OK.

 When Windows XP is downloading updates to your computer, it doesn't interrupt your work. The download happens in the background of other work you're doing, and you can even download more than one file at a time.

 You can also go to the Windows Update Web site by opening the Help & Support Center (choose Start➪Help and Support) and clicking the Windows Update link in the Resources on the left. Windows Update is also available from the Start➪All Programs menu.

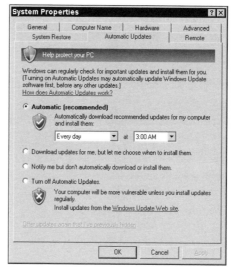

Figure 9-9: The System Properties dialog box, Automatic Updates tab

 If you happen to disconnect or lose your connection to the Internet before an update finishes downloading, don't panic. The next time you go online, Windows Update completes the download right from where you left off.

Working with Files and Folders

Whereas important data was once kept in metal filing cabinets and manila file folders, most data is now stored in sleek computer workstations and on network and Web servers.

Windows-based PCs still organize the work you do every day in files and folders, but the metal and cardboard have been dropped in favor of electronic bits and bytes. *Files* are the individual documents that you save from within applications such as Word and Excel. You use *folders* and *subfolders* to organize sets of files into groups or categories, such as by project or by customer.

In this chapter, you find out how to organize and work with files and folders, including:

➠ **Finding your way around files and folders:** This includes tasks such as locating and opening files and folders.

➠ **Squeezing a file's contents:** This is where you hear all about creating a compressed folder to reduce a large file to a more manageable size so you can save space on your computer, or more easily e-mail it to somebody else.

➠ **Manipulating files and folders:** These tasks cover moving, renaming, deleting, and printing a file.

Chapter 10

Get ready to . . .

Locate Files and Folders in My Computer

1. Choose Start➪My Computer.

2. In the My Computer window (see Figure 10-1) double-click a drive, such as a floppy, CD-ROM, or computer hard drive to access it.

3. In the resulting window (see Figure 10-2 for an example), double-click the folder (or a series of folders) until you locate it. If the file that you want is stored within a folder, double-click the folder (or a series of folders) until you locate it.

4. When you find the file you want, double-click it to open it.

 Note the File and Folder Tasks area on the left side of the window in Figure 10-2. Use the commands in this area to perform common file and folder tasks, such as e-mailing a file or folder, copying it, deleting it, or moving it.

 Depending on how you choose to display files and folders, you might see file/folder listings — as in Figure 10-2 — or icons or even thumbnail representations of file contents.

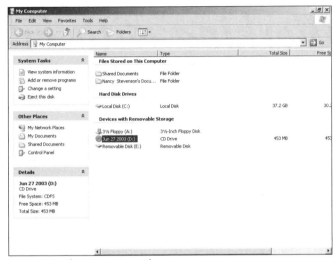

Figure 10-1: The My Computer window

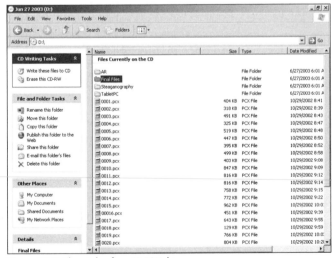

Figure 10-2: The window for a CD-ROM drive

Locate Files and Folders in Windows Explorer

1. Choose Start⟶All Programs⟶Accessories⟶Windows Explorer.

2. In the Windows Explorer window, as shown in Figure 10-3, double-click the folder or click the plus sign to the left of a folder in the Folders pane along the left side to obtain the file inside the folder.

3. The folder's contents are shown on the right in Explorer. If necessary, open a series of folders in this manner until you locate the file you want.

4. When you find the file you want, double-click it to open it.

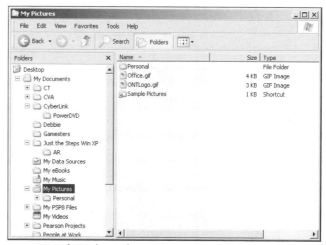

Figure 10-3: The Windows Explorer window

 To see different perspectives and information about files in Windows Explorer, click the arrow on the View button (it looks like a little window with blue title bar across the top) and choose one of the following menu options: Thumbnails (graphical representations of file contents); Tiles or Icons (folder and file icons in different arrangements); List (a list of file and folder names with small icon symbols); or Details (adds file type and size to the file list).

 If you have trouble finding the file or folder you want, consider changing the view by clicking the View button on the My Documents window to show information such as file size and date last modified. This might help you identify the specific file you want.

Search for a File

1. Choose Start⇨Search.

2. In the resulting Search Results window, click the arrow for the type of item for which you want to search (for example, Pictures, Music, or Video, or Documents).

3. In the resulting window (see Figure 10-4), select any of the criteria, enter a word or phrase to search by, and then click the Search button.

4. Click the Sort Results by Category or View Results Differently arrows to get a different perspective on your results:

   - **Sort Results by Category** (see Figure 10-5): Sort results by name, date last modified, size, or file type.

   - **View Results Differently:** Select different graphical or text representations of results, such as thumbnails or details.

5. Click any of the arrows under Refine This Search to search again if you don't find the file you want.

6. When you locate the file you want, double-click it to open it.

 When you're in the Search Results window in Step 2 (where you choose the type of file to search for), click the Use Advanced Search Options button to find additional search options, including a keyword feature for words or phrases contained within documents, a field to specify the search location, and a way to specify file size.

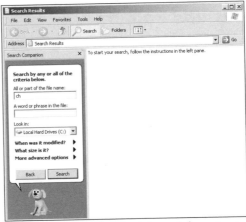

Figure 10-4: The Search Results window ready for you to enter search criteria

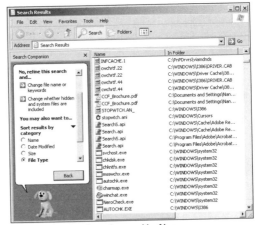

Figure 10-5: Search results sorted by file type

Launch a Recently Used Document

1. Choose Start and right-click any blank area in the Start menu or the title bar.

2. In the resulting shortcut menu, choose Properties.

3. In the Properties dialog box that appears, click the Start Menu tab (if that tab isn't already displayed) and then click the active Customize button (the button related to the style of Start menu you are using, Windows XP or Classic).

4. In the Customize Start Menu dialog box, display the Advanced tab (see Figure 10-6).

5. Make sure that the List My Most Recently Opened Documents check box is selected and then click OK.

6. Choose Start⇨My Recent Documents and then click a file in the resulting submenu (see Figure 10-7) to open it.

 If a file in the My Recent Documents list can be opened with more than one application — for example, a graphics file that you might open with Paint or Windows Picture and Fax Viewer — you can right-click the file and use the Open With command to control which application you use to open the file.

Figure 10-6: The Advanced tab in the Customize Start Menu dialog box

Figure 10-7: The My Recent Documents item that now appears on the Start menu

Create a Shortcut to a File or Folder

1. Locate the file or folder by using Windows Explorer. (Choose Start⊏>All Programs⊏>Accessories⊏>Windows Explorer.)

2. In the resulting Windows Explorer window (see Figure 10-8), right-click the file or folder that you want to create a shortcut for and then choose Create Shortcut.

3. A shortcut named Shortcut to File or Folder Name appears at the bottom of the open folder. Click the shortcut and drag it to the desktop.

 To open the file in its originating application or a folder in Windows Explorer, simply double-click the desktop shortcut icon.

 A shortcut listed on your Start menu will have (2) after the program name. On your desktop, a shortcut icon will have a small white box with a black arrow in the bottom left corner.

 Don't clutter your desktop up too much with shortcuts or you'll have trouble finding the things. Just put the programs or documents you use most often there and keep your desktop neat.

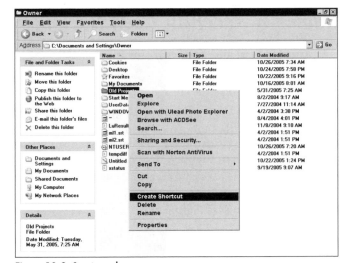

Figure 10-8: Creating a shortcut

Create a Compressed Folder

1. Locate the files or folders that you want to compress by using Windows Explorer. (Choose Start⇨All Programs⇨ Accessories⇨Windows Explorer.)

2. In the resulting Windows Explorer window, you can do the following:

   - **Select individual or consecutive files or folders.** Click a file or folder, press and hold Shift to select a series of items listed consecutively in the folder, and click the final item.

   - **Select nonconsecutive files or folders.** Press the Ctrl key and click the items (as shown in Figure 10-9).

3. Right-click selected items; in the resulting shortcut menu (see Figure 10-10), choose Send To⇨Compressed (Zipped) Folder. A new compressed folder appears. The folder icon is named after the last file you selected in the series.

 Windows XP will name the compressed folder after the last file you selected in a set of files. Because this file name is unlikely to make it clear what the whole set of files is, you can rename a compressed folder with a name other than the one that Windows XP automatically assigns to it. See the task "Rename a File or Folder" in this chapter to find out just how to do that.

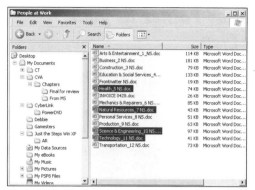

Figure 10-9: Selecting a series of nonconsecutive files and folders

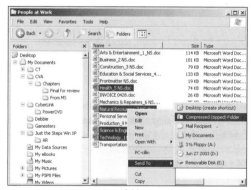

Figure 10-10: Compressing a folder

Add a File or Folder to Your Favorites List

1. Open Windows Explorer. (Choose Start⇨All Programs⇨ Windows Explorer).

2. In the resulting Windows Explorer window, click a file or folder and choose Favorites⇨Add to Favorites.

3. In the dialog box that appears, enter a name to be displayed in the Favorites list for the file or folder and then click OK. (See Figure 10-11.)

4. To open a Favorite, choose Start⇨Favorites (see Figure 10-12) and click an item from the submenu to open it.

 To see a list of your Favorites, choose Start⇨Favorites.

 If the Favorites item doesn't display on your Start menu, right-click the Start menu and choose Properties. On the Start Menu tab with Start Menu selected, click the Customize button. Click the Advanced tab to display it, make sure that Favorites is selected, and then click OK twice to save the setting.

Figure 10-11: The AddFavorite dialog box

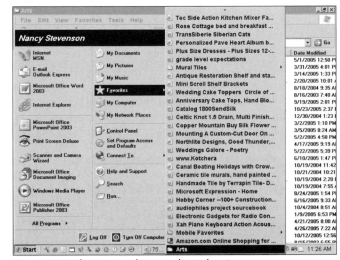

Figure 10-12: The Favorites submenu on the Windows Start menu

Move a File or Folder

1. Choose Start⇨All Programs⇨Accessories⇨Windows Explorer.

2. In the resulting Windows Explorer window, double-click a folder or series of folders to locate the file that you want to move, or if you want to move an entire folder, locate and select that folder.

3. Do one of the following actions:

- Click and drag the file or folder to another folder in the Folders pane on the left side of the window. If you right-click and drag, you are offered the options of moving or copying the item when you place it via a *Smart Tag* (a floating menu list of options that appears when you release your mouse button) (see Figure 10-13).

- Right-click the file or folder and choose Send To. Then choose from the options shown in the sub-menu that appears (shown in Figure 10-14).

4. Click the Close button in the upper-right corner of the Windows Explorer window to close it.

 To view files or folders on your storage media (such as your CD-ROM drive), scroll to the bottom of the Folders pane in Windows Explorer and click My Computer. You see your hard drive and any removable storage media displayed in the right pane. Double-click any item to display the files and folders contained there.

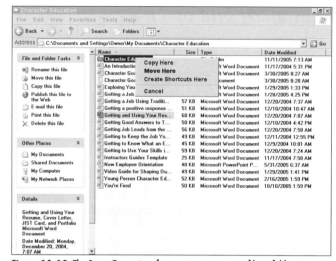

Figure 10-13: The Smart Tag options for moving or copying a file or folder

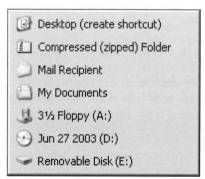

Figure 10-14: The Send To submenu

Rename a File or Folder

1. Locate the file that you want to rename by using Windows Explorer. (Choose Start⇨All Programs⇨ Accessories⇨Windows Explorer.)

2. Right-click the file and choose Rename (see Figure 10-15).

3. The filename is now available for editing. Type a new name and then click anywhere outside the filename to save the new name.

 You can't rename a file to have the same name as another file located in the same folder. To give a file the same name as another, cut it from its current location, paste it into another folder, and then follow the procedure in this task. Or, open the file and save it to a new location with the same name, which creates a copy.

 You can't rename a file which is currently open. First, close the file, and then do the procedure above. Also, you cannot use certain characters such as \ /, :, *, <, >, and | in a file name.

 If you want to rename a file in a folder that contains a file with the same name, Windows won't allow you to do it. Instead, copy the file, paste it in another folder, rename it using the procedures in this task, and then cut and paste the file back into the original folder.

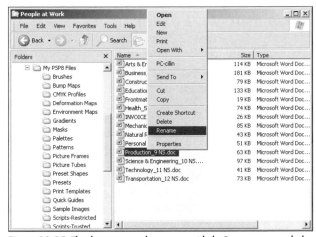

Figure 10-15: The shortcut menu that appears with the Rename command when you right-click a file or folder

Print a File

1. Open the file in the application that it was created in.

2. Choose File⇨Print.

3. In the resulting Print dialog box (see Figure 10-16) select what to print; these options might vary, but generally include:

- **All** prints all pages in the document.

- **Current Page** prints whatever page your cursor is active in at the moment.

- **Pages** prints a page range or series of pages you enter in that field. For example, enter **3–11** to print pages 3 through 11, or enter **3, 7, 9–11** to print pages 3, 7, and 9 through 11.

- **Selection** prints any text or objects that you have selected with your cursor when you choose the Print command.

4. In the Copies field, click the up or down arrow (or type in a number) to set the number of copies to make; if you want multiple copies collated, select the Collate check box.

5. Click the OK button to proceed with printing.

 Here's another method for printing. Locate the file by using Windows Explorer (choose Start⇨All Programs⇨Accessories⇨Windows Explorer). Right-click the file and choose Print from the shortcut menu that appears (see Figure 10-8). The file prints with your default printer settings.

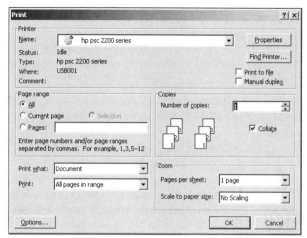

Figure 10-16: The Print dialog box

 Different applications might offer different options in the Print dialog box. For example, PowerPoint offers several options for what to print, including slides, handouts, or the presentation outline, and Outlook allows you to print e-mails in table or memo styles.

Delete a File or Folder

1. Locate the file or folder by using Windows Explorer. (Choose Start⇨All Programs⇨Accessories⇨Windows Explorer.)

2. In the resulting Windows Explorer window, right-click the file or folder that you want to delete and then choose Delete.

3. In the resulting dialog box (see Figure 10-17), click Yes to delete the file.

 When you delete a file or folder in Windows XP it's not really gone. It's removed to the Recycle Bin. Windows XP periodically purges older files from the Recycle Bin, but you might still be able to retrieve recently deleted files and folders from it. To try to restore a deleted file or folder, double-click the Recycle Bin icon on the desktop. Right-click the file or folder and choose Restore. Windows XP restores the file to the drive and folder from where it was deleted.

 A shortcut to deleting a file or folder is to right-click on the file or folder in Windows Explorer and choose Delete.

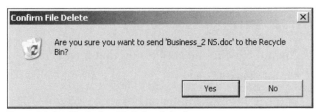

Figure 10-17: The Confirm File Delete dialog box

 Don't use this procedure to delete an entire program. That may not delete the various files that the program installed in the system. Instead, choose Start⇨Control Panel⇨Add/Remove Programs and use the tools there to delete the program.

Exploring Windows Assets

*W*indows XP isn't just a control center for your computer's hardware and other software programs; it has its own set of neat tools that you can use to get your work done. What sorts of things? Well, by using various Windows Accessories (that is, built-in software programs), you can do everything from writing down great thoughts to working with beautiful pictures. Here's what Windows' built-in applications help you to do:

⟶ **Get assistance with your computer.** Windows provides several options for getting important computer updates and help with your computing experience.

⟶ **Work with words.** *WordPad* is a program that provides a virtual notepad for jotting down ideas, making notes, creating small documents, or entering programming code. WordPad is a no-bells-and-whistles word processor.

⟶ **Manipulate numbers.** The Windows Calculator doesn't fit in the palm of your hand, but it does offer a little onscreen calculator. Enter numbers by using your mouse or keyboard. WordPad can handle even complex calculations.

⟶ **Play with images.** Windows XP makes you an artist by letting you view and edit graphics files in Paint. You can view digital images (you know, the photos you took at little Cindy's swim meet?) in Windows Picture and Fax Viewer. You can also control what images appear on your Windows desktop background.

⟶ **Manage contacts and communicate.** The Windows Address Book is an electronic version of that little alphabetical book you keep by your phone; it's a great place to store contact information. Windows Messenger is an instant messaging program that allows you to chat online in real-time.

Chapter

11

Get ready to . . .

Explore Help Topics

1. Choose Start⇨Help and Support to open the Support Center, as shown in Figure 11-1. *Note:* If your copy of Windows XP came built into your computer, some computer manufacturers (such as Hewlett-Packard) customize this center to add information that's specific to your computer system.

2. Click a help topic link in the Pick a Help Topic column to display the next level of options. Along the left side of the following screen, you see major topics listed, some of them with a plus sign to the left.

3. Click any of the plus signs to expand the topic and see a list of subtopics. Eventually you get down to the deepest level of detailed subtopics, as shown in Figure 11-2.

4. Click a topic in the Pick a Task list on the right to display the topic. When you get to this level, you might find additional links to display information about various aspects of this topic, links within the help text that you can click to get background information or definitions of terms, and a Related Topics area where you click links to take you to other information related to the topic.

5. When you finish reading about the topic(s), click the Close button to close the Help and Support Center window.

 At the topic level, a See Also list box is available on the left that provides links to other useful resources. For example, from any list of topics, you can access a glossary of computer terms that might help you understand what's being explained by the Help and Support Center, or you can click a link to go to a related newsgroup or get a list of Windows keystroke shortcuts.

Figure 11-1: Microsoft's Help and Support Center

Figure 11-2: Detailed level help topics

Search for Help

1. Open the Help and Support Center.

2. Enter a search term in the Search box and click the Search button (the red button with an arrow to the right of the Search box). Search results, such as those shown in Figure 11-3, appear.

3. Explore the results by clicking various links in the Search Results area on the left. These links offer a few different types of results:

   - The **Suggested Topics** list offers help topics, articles, and tutorials related to your search.

   - The **Full-Text Search Matches** area lists links to more help topics.

   - The **Microsoft Knowledge Base** list offers related technical articles from the Microsoft Web site.

4. Click any item to display it. If you have no luck, enter a different search term in the Search text box and start again.

5. To change how Search operates, click the Set Search Options link under the Search text box. You can change the following settings:

   - Change the number of results returned in the Return Up To *xx* Results Per Provider text box at the top. (The default is 15, as shown in Figure 11-4.)

   - Select the Turn on Search Highlight check box to turn this feature on so that instances of the search term are highlighted in the results.

   - Select a check box to select or deselect one of the three search results options.

6. In the Search For drop-down list (scroll down to see this feature), choose how the search should be performed: for example, based on all words in the search phrase, based on any of the words, or based only by the exact phrase you enter.

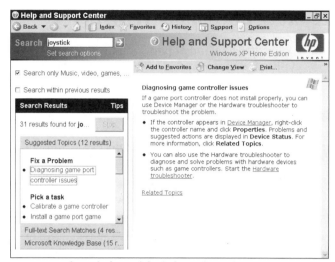

Figure 11-3: The result of a search for the keyword *joystick*

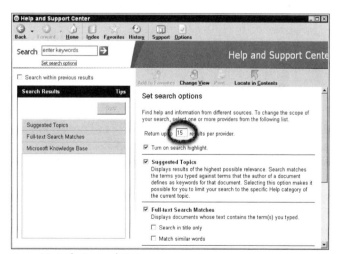

Figure 11-4: The Set Search Options page

Connect to Remote Assistance

1. Open the Help and Support Center. Click the Remote Assistance link in the Ask for Assistance area of the Help and Support Center.

2. On the Remote Assistance page, as shown in Figure 11-5, click the Remote Assistance link. On the page that appears (see Figure 11-6), you can notify any helpful friend or associate whom you can contact through Windows Messenger that you want them to help you.

3. You can use Windows Messenger or e-mail to invite somebody to help you. For these steps, fill in an e-mail address and then click the Invite This Person button.

4. On the E-Mail an Invitation page, enter your name in the From text box and type a message in the Message text box, and then click Continue.

5. On the resulting page, set a time limit on the invitation and require that the recipient use a password to access your computer remotely (a wise security measure). Use the drop-down lists in the Set the Invitation to Expire area to set the time that you want the invitation to last.

 Setting a time limit of no more than a few hours is a good idea. After all, you don't want somebody trying to log on to your computer unexpectedly two weeks from now when you've already solved the problem some other way.

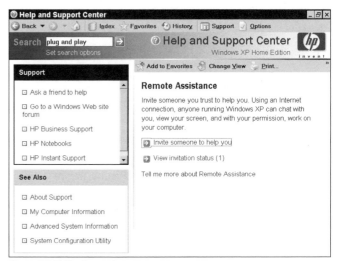

Figure 11-5: The Remote Assistance page

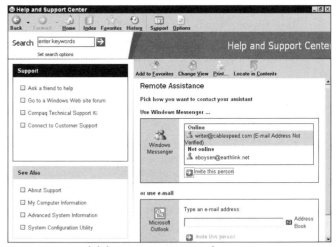

Figure 11-6: Invite help by instant message or e-mail

6. If you want to require a password, enter it and confirm it.

 Remember, it's up to you to let the recipient know the password — it isn't included in your e-mail. If you don't want to use a password, be sure to deselect the check box for this option before continuing.

7. Click the Send Invitation button. The recipient receives an e-mail that includes any message you entered, a standard Remote Assistance message, and a link to further instructions, as shown in Figure 11-7.

8. At this point, the recipient should open the `MsRcIncident` file attached to the e-mail, and if prompted, open it rather than save it. The recipient clicks Yes to accept the invitation and then enters a password, if required.

9. If you're online, you see a message from your remote buddy asking whether you want this person to view your screen and chat. You can initiate the connection by clicking Yes. You can chat online, and the person helping you can even take over your mouse and keyboard and work with your computer (with your permission) by using the tools shown in Figure 11-8.

- Use the Take Control/Stop Control button to allow the person to take over your system and stop him/her when assistance is no longer needed.

- Enter a message and click Send to communicate.

- Use the Send a File button to share files that might help or be causing problems for you.

10. When you're done with your session, click the Disconnect button.

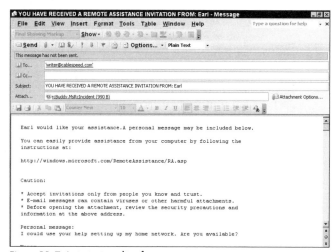

Figure 11-7: An invitation asking for assistance

Figure 11-8: The control screen for a Remote Assistance session

Manage Windows Updates

1. Choose Start⇨Control Panel⇨Performance and Maintenance⇨System.

2. In the System Properties dialog box, click the Automatic Updates tab to display it (see Figure 11-9).

3. Select one of the four radio buttons to specify how you want to manage updates:

   • **Automatic:** Downloads and installs updates at the specified frequency and time of day you select from the two drop-down list boxes here.

   • **Download Updates For Me:** Lets updates download but not install until you choose to do so.

   • **Notify Me:** Causes Windows to send you a message that downloads are available, but they are not down-loaded or installed.

   • **Turn Off Automatic Updates:** Turns this feature off entirely. To get updates, you have to go to the Windows Update Web site, which you can do by clicking the link at this radio button.

4. Click OK.

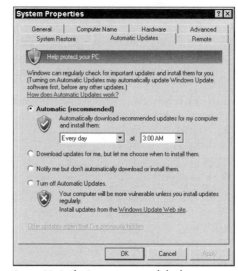

Figure 11-9: The System Properties dialog box, Automatic Updates tab

 When Windows is downloading updates to your computer, it doesn't interrupt your work. The download happens in the background of other work you're doing, and you can even download other files at the same time.

 You can also go to the Windows Update Web site by opening the Help and Support Center (choose Start⇨Help and Support) and clicking the Windows Update link in the Resources area on the left. Windows Update is also listed when you choose Start⇨All Programs.

 If you happen to disconnect or lose your connection to the Internet before an update finishes downloading, don't panic. The next time you go online, Windows Update completes the download right from where you left off.

Create and Format a Document in WordPad

1. Choose Start➪All Programs➪Accessories➪WordPad.

2. Enter text in the blank document. (**Note:** Press Enter to create blank lines between paragraphs.)

3. Click and drag to select the text, and then choose Format➪Font.

4. In the resulting Font dialog box, as shown in Figure 11-10, adjust the settings for Font, Font Style, or Size; apply strikeout (strikethrough) or underline effects by selecting those check boxes. You can also modify the font color. Click OK to apply the settings (see Figure 11-11).

5. Select text and click various other tools, such as the alignment buttons or the bullet style button on the toolbar to format selected text.

6. When your document is complete, choose File➪Save. In the Save As dialog box, enter a name in the File Name text box, select a file location from the Save In drop-down list, and then click Save.

 E-mailing a copy of your WordPad document to a friend is simple. Just choose File➪Send, and an e-mail form appears from your default e-mail program with the file already attached. Just enter a recipient and a message and then click Send. It's on its way!

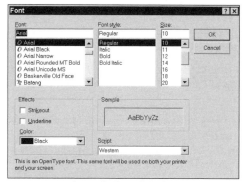

Figure 11-10: The WordPad Font dialog box

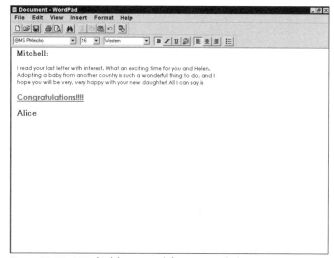

Figure 11-11: A WordPad document with formatting applied to text

Use the Windows Calculator

1. Choose Start⇨All Programs⇨Accessories⇨Calculator.

2. In the resulting Calculator window (as shown in Figure 11-12), you can enter numbers and symbols in a few different ways:

   • Type numbers and symbols on your keyboard using either number keys or the numeric keypad, which appear in the entry box of the calculator. Then press Enter to perform the calculation.

   • Click numbers or symbols on the calculator display and then click the = button to perform the calculation.

3. When you don't need Calculator anymore, you have two options:

   • Click the Minimize button to shrink the window to the taskbar. (Simply click the taskbar Calculator icon to maximize Calculator.)

   • Click the Close button to close the window. To open it again, you have to go through the Start menu.

 To enter the mathematical operators in your calculations using only keyboard entries you have to know the correct symbols to use. For example, to divide 22 by 2, type **22/2** and then press Enter. Use the plus, minus, and asterisk (multiply) symbols in this same way.

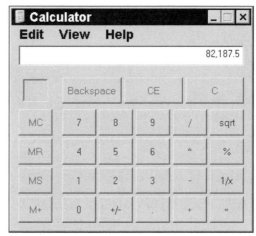

Figure 11-12: The Calculator window

 If you're the scientific type, try displaying the scientific calculator by choosing View⇨Scientific. Now you can play with things that are Greek to me, like cosines, logarithms, and pi. (Okay, I know what pi is; it goes on forever, just like a politician's promise.) With the Scientific view displayed, additional choices become available on the View menu, such as changing from decimal to binary or degrees to radians. Math geeks, rejoice!

Choose a Desktop Background

1. Right-click the desktop and choose Properties from the shortcut menu that appears.

2. In the resulting Display Properties dialog box, click the Desktop tab to display it, as shown in Figure 11-13.

3. Select a desktop background option from the Background list.

4. From the Position drop-down list box, select one of the following options:

   - **Center:** Centers the image on a colored background so that you can see a border of color around its edges.

   - **Tile:** Displays multiple copies of the image filling the desktop. The number of images depends on the size and resolution of the original graphic.

   - **Stretch:** This stretches the image to cover your entire screen; this may distort certain images depending on their original proportions.

5. Click the arrow for the Color drop-down list to display a palette of colors. (This color is visible if you select the Center position setting.) Click a color in the palette or click the Other button to see a larger spectrum of colors to choose from.

6. Click the Apply button to apply the settings and see what they look like, or just click OK to apply the settings and close the dialog box. Figure 11-14 shows the setting applied.

 If you don't want an image on your desktop, choose None for your background and then choose a color from the Color drop-down palette. If you don't like the colors offered, you can access a whole range of colors by clicking the Other button in the Color palette.

Figure 11-13: The Display Properties dialog box, Desktop tab

Figure 11-14: A new background displayed on the desktop

Edit a Picture in Paint

1. Choose Start➪All Programs➪Accessories➪Paint.

2. In the resulting Paint window, choose File➪Open. Locate a picture file that you want to edit (as in Figure 11-15), select it, and then click Open. A pretty picture of my kitten is shown in the Paint window in Figure 11-16.

3. Now you can edit the picture in any number of ways:

   - **Edit colors.** Choose a color from the color palette in the bottom-left corner and use various tools (such as Airbrush, Brush, Fill With Color, and the Color Dropper) to apply color to the image or selected drawn objects, such as rectangles.

   - **Select areas.** Select the Free-Form Select and Select tools, and then click and drag on the image to select portions of the picture. You can then crop out these elements by choosing Edit➪Cut.

   - **Add text.** Select the Text tool, and then click and drag the image to create a text box in which you can enter and format text.

   - **Draw objects.** Select the Rectangle, Rounded Rectangle, Polygon, or Ellipse tool, and then click and drag the image to draw objects.

   - **Modify the image.** Use the commands on the Image menu to change the colors and stretch out, flip around, or change the size of the image.

4. Choose File➪Save to save your masterpiece, choose File➪Print to print it, or choose File➪Send to send it by e-mail.

Figure 11-15: The Open dialog box

Figure 11-16: A picture opened in Paint

Use the Windows Picture and Fax Viewer

1. Locate an image file on your hard drive, network, or storage media by using Windows Explorer. (Choose Start⇨All Programs⇨Accessories⇨Windows Explorer.)

2. Right-click the filename or icon and choose Open With⇨Windows Picture and Fax Viewer. In the resulting Windows Picture and Fax Viewer window, as shown in Figure 11-17, you can use the tools at the bottom to do any of the following:

- The Next Image and Previous Image icons move to a previous or following image in the same folder.

- The Best Fit and Actual Size icons modify the display of the image in the Picture and Fax Viewer.

- The Start Slide Show icon begins a full-screen slide show of the currently open image.

- The Zoom In and Zoom Out icons enlarge or shrink the image display.

- The Rotate Clockwise and Rotate Counterclockwise icons spin the image 90 degrees at a time (see Figure 11-18).

- Delete, Print, Copy To, and Close All do what their names say.

- Save or Send images to others.

3. When you finish viewing images, click the Close button in the top-right corner to close the Viewer.

Figure 11-17: Windows Picture and Fax Viewer

Figure 11-18: A rotated image

Enter Contacts in the Windows Address Book

1. Choose Start➪All Programs➪Accessories➪Address Book. You might get a dialog box asking whether you want to make this your default vCard (an electronic business card) viewer. Click Yes or No depending on your preference.

2. In the Address Book window (as shown in Figure 11-19), click the New button and select New Contact from the drop-down list that appears.

3. In the *Contact Name* Properties dialog box that appears (see Figure 11-20), enter information in various fields, clicking other tabs to add more details. For some fields, such as E-Mail Addresses, you must enter information and then click the Add button to add it to your list.

4. When you finish entering information, click OK.

 If the contact has more than one e-mail address, select the one you want to most often send e-mail to and click the Set as Default button. This is the address any e-mails to that contact will be addressed to.

 To quickly search your Address Book, choose Start➪Search, click the Other Search Options link, and then click the Computers or People link in the Search window. To start your search, click the link labeled People in Your Address Book. You can then define criteria, such as address, phone number, or e-mail address, to search by.

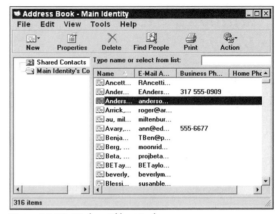

Figure 11-19: Windows Address Book

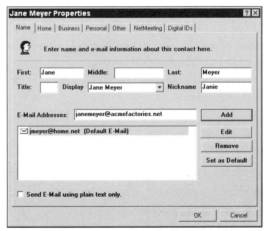

Figure 11-20: Entering new contact information

Add a Contact to Windows Messenger

1. Choose Start➪All Programs➪Windows Messenger.

2. In the Windows Messenger window, click the Click Here to Sign In link. If you don't have a .NET Passport (a sign-in credential used by MSN Messenger and other Microsoft services that speeds up your sign-in to certain services), you will be prompted to sign up for one. Enter required information in the series of screens that appears. (If you already have a passport, you sign in automatically and can skip this step.)

3. Click the Add a Contact link in the Windows Messenger window, as shown in Figure 11-21.

4. In the Add a Contact dialog box that appears, click Next to accept the default option of entering your contact's information.

5. In the next Add a Contact dialog box, enter the person's e-mail address and then click Next. Note that the person must have a .NET Passport to be accepted as a Windows Messenger contact.

6. In the Windows Messenger dialog box that appears, select one of the two radio buttons and then click OK:

   • Allow this person to see when you are online and contact you.

   • Block this person from seeing when you are online and contacting you.

7. To send an e-mail notifying the contact about how to install Windows Messenger, click the Send E-mail button (see Figure 11-22) and enter any personal message in the resulting e-mail form.

8. Click Next and then click Cancel to close the wizard. (Or, if you click Next at this point, you begin the process all over again to add another contact.)

Figure 11-21: The initial Windows Messenger window

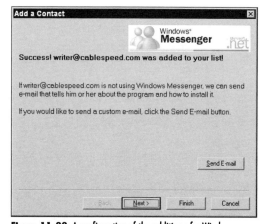

Figure 11-22: A confirmation of the addition of a Windows Messenger contact

Part III
Working with Your Display, Multimedia, and Graphics

Setting Up Your Display

Your monitor is your window into the world of your computer. It's where you view all the data and images your PC stores and manipulates. Essentially three elements are involved in what you see on your monitor screen: the monitor itself, the graphics card installed in your CPU, and the *driver* (that is, software) that controls your monitor.

In addition to these three items, it's important to know how to make settings to fine-tune your display so it's easy on your eyes, especially if you work on your computer many hours every day.

To customize your display, you can do the following:

➡ **Make settings for your monitor and display.** Windows XP provides settings that you can use to set up your monitor and control the driver as well as various features, such as how often the screen image refreshes. You can also add a new graphics card to provide up-to-date capabilities for your display.

➡ **Change how the desktop looks.** Set up Windows XP to display images and colors. You can also use screen saver settings to switch from everyday work stuff to a pretty animation when you've stopped working for a time.

➡ **Connect your desktop to the online world.** *Active Desktop*, the feature of Windows XP that allows you to keep a live Internet site on your desktop, is a mixed blessing. It can keep you constantly in tune with what's going on in the world while slowing down your computer as it chomps up computer power like a person eating popcorn at a movie. Whether it's a feature you want to use or not, this chapter helps you set up Active Desktop to see whether it's a good fit for you.

Chapter 12

Get ready to . . .

Enable Usage of a Monitor

1. Right-click the desktop and choose Properties from the resulting menu.

2. In the Display dialog box that appears, click the Settings tab and then click the Advanced button.

3. In the Advanced dialog box (see Figure 12-1), click the Monitor tab and then click the Properties button.

4. On the General tab of the Monitor Properties dialog box (see Figure 12-2), click the arrow in the Device Usage drop-down list and choose Use This Device (Enable).

5. Click OK three times to close all dialog boxes and save the new setting.

 A monitor should be disabled only if it is causing system problems. A plug-and-play monitor should be enabled automatically when you install its driver and plug it in. If you or somebody else has cause to disable the monitor, you can use this procedure to enable it again.

 Before you disable a monitor device consider trying to solve your problem first. Click the Troubleshoot button in the General tab of the Monitor Properties dialog box, and follow the instructions there to pin down the problem.

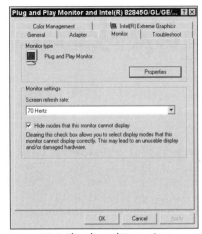

Figure 12-1: The Advanced Monitor Settings dialog box

Figure 12-2: The Monitor Properties dialog box

Update Your Monitor Driver

1. Right-click the desktop and choose Properties from the resulting menu.

2. In the Display dialog box that appears, click the Settings tab and then click the Advanced button.

3. In the Advanced dialog box, click the Monitor tab and then click the Properties button.

4. On the Driver tab (see Figure 12-3) of the Monitor Properties dialog box, click the Update Driver button.

5. In the Hardware Update Wizard that appears, choose Yes, This Time Only; then click Next.

6. In the next wizard window (see Figure 12-4), choose one of two options, depending on whether you have a CD with the driver on it or you downloaded the driver file to another location. Click Next.

7. Depending on your choice in Step 6, either:

   • An additional dialog box appears, allowing you to specify a location for the driver; then click Next to proceed.

   • Or the driver installs from the CD.

8. In the final wizard window that appears, click Finish.

9. Click OK three times to close all dialog boxes and save the new setting.

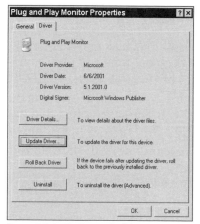

Figure 12-3: The Driver tab of the Monitor Properties dialog box

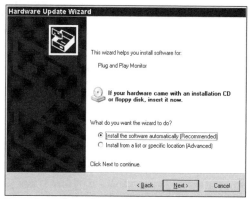

Figure 12-4: The Hardware Update Wizard

Install a New Graphics Card

1. First, uninstall the existing graphics card driver by using the Add Or Remove Programs feature of the Control Panel. (See Chapter 9 for more about removing software.)

2. Shut off your computer and unplug it. Also shut off any peripherals attached to it, such as a printer, and disconnect your monitor from the CPU (computer body).

3. Remove your CPU cover following the directions in your computer manual. Before touching anything inside the CPU, touch a piece of metal to get rid of any static discharge.

4. Locate the current graphics card (using your manual if necessary) and remove it (see Figure 12-5). This might involve unscrewing the card with a Philips screwdriver.

5. Position the new graphics card over the slot and insert it firmly but gently (see Figure 12-6). If you removed a card-holder screw in Step 4, replace it.

6. Replace the computer cover and plug your monitor back in. Turn on your monitor and then your computer. Your computer automatically detects the new card and displays the Found New Hardware Wizard. Follow its directions to install the new driver.

Whenever you open the your computer case, be very careful about static discharge, which can harm you and the delicate electronics in your computer. Consider wearing an antistatic wristband, which you can get at most electronics stores. Also, to cut down on static, stand on a rubber mat rather than on a shag carpet. Finally, occasionally touch a piece of metal to discharge any static in your body.

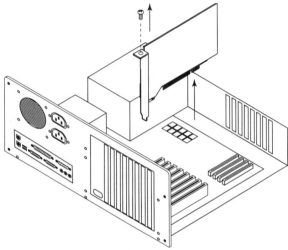

Figure 12-5: Removing a graphics card.

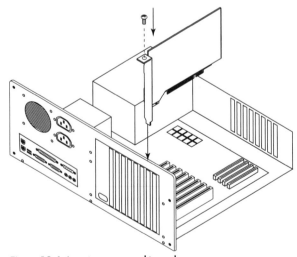

Figure 12-6: Inserting a new graphics card

Change the DPI Setting

1. Right-click the desktop and choose Properties from the resulting menu.

2. In the Display dialog box that appears, click the Settings tab and then click the Advanced button (see Figure 12-7).

3. In the Advanced dialog box on the General tab (see Figure 12-8), click the DPI Setting arrow and select Normal Size or Large Size.

4. A message box appears explaining that any changes to fonts will appear after they are installed and the computer is restarted. Click OK to close the message.

5. Click OK twice to save the setting and close the dialog boxes.

 DPI stands for *dots per inch*. The DPI Setting list includes all DPI settings available for your particular monitor. Using a larger DPI setting (more dots per inch) makes everything you see on your screen larger.

 Changing your screen resolution has a similar affect to changing the DPI but relates to the image on your monitor, not the printed image. See the later task, Set Your Screen Resolution for more about this.

Figure 12-7: The Display dialog box, Settings tab

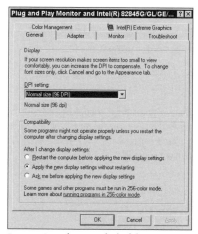

Figure 12-8: The General tab of the Monitor Properties dialog box

Adjust Your Computer's Refresh Rate

1. Right-click the desktop and choose Properties from the resulting menu.

2. In the Display dialog box that appears, click the Settings tab and then click the Advanced button.

3. In the Advanced dialog box, click the Monitor tab (see Figure 12-9), click the Screen Refresh Rate arrow, and choose a different refresh rate.

4. Click Apply. A message box appears (see Figure 12-10) stating that your desktop is being reconfigured and asking whether you want to keep the settings. Click Yes (if you don't respond within a number of seconds the settings will be saved).

5. Click OK to close the Display dialog box.

 The Refresh Rate list includes all settings available for your particular monitor. Using a larger setting causes your monitor to have less flicker, which is an effect that is more visible when the refresh happens less frequently.

 Check your monitor documentation to see how high a refresh rate it will support. By default Windows sets the refresh rate at 100 Hertz. If your monitor allows a higher setting, you may want to select it to reduce flicker as much as possible.

Figure 12-9: The Monitor tab of the Advanced Display dialog box

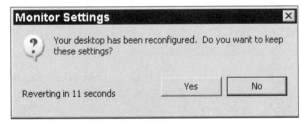

Figure 12-10: Confirming your refresh rate

Set Your Screen's Resolution

1. Right-click the desktop to display a shortcut menu and then choose Properties.

2. In the resulting Display Properties dialog box, as shown in Figure 12-11, click the Settings tab.

3. On the Settings tab, move the slider in the Screen Resolution area to a higher or lower resolution.

4. Click OK to accept the new screen resolution.

Higher resolutions, such as 1400 x 1250, produce smaller, crisper images. Lower resolutions, such as 800 x 600, produce larger, somewhat jagged images. The upside of higher resolution is that more fits on your screen; the downside is that words and graphics can be hard to see. One option: If fonts appear too small to read, change the Font Size setting on the Appearance tab of the Display Properties dialog box to be Large or Extra Large.

Another way to improve the quality of what you see on your monitor is to adjust the Color Quality setting on the Settings tab of the Display Properties dialog box. Lower color quality is 16 bit; highest is 32 bit. Essentially the higher the bits, the more color definition you get.

Figure 12-11: The Display Properties dialog box, Settings tab

Remember that you can also use your View settings in most software programs to get a larger or smaller view of your documents without having to change your screen's resolution.

Change the Desktop Image

1. Right-click the desktop and choose Properties from the shortcut menu.

2. In the resulting Display Properties dialog box, click the Desktop tab to display it, as shown in Figure 12-12.

3. Select a desktop background option from the Background list box.

4. From the Position drop-down list, select one of the following options:

    -   **Center:** Quite logically, this option centers the image on a colored background so that you can see a border of color around its edges.

    -   **Tile:** This choice displays multiple copies of the image filling the desktop. The number of images depends on the size and resolution of the original graphic.

    -   **Stretch:** This option stretches one copy of the image to fill the screen, covering any background color completely.

5. Click the arrow for the Color drop-down list to display a palette of colors. (This option is visible if you select the Center position setting.) Click a color in the palette or click the Other button to see a larger spectrum of colors to choose from.

6. Click the Apply button to apply the settings to see what they look like, or just click OK to apply the settings and close the dialog box. Figure 12-13 shows the setting applied.

 If you apply a desktop theme (see more about this in Chapter 11), you overwrite whatever desktop settings you've made in this task. If you apply a desktop theme and then go back and make desktop settings, you'll replace the theme's settings. But making changes is easy and it keeps your desktop interesting, so play around with themes and desktop backgrounds all you like!

Figure 12-12: The Display Properties dialog box, Desktop tab

Figure 12-13: A desktop image setting applied

Enable Active Desktop

1. Right-click the desktop and choose Properties. Click the Desktop tab and then click the Customize Desktop button.

2. In the resulting Desktop Items dialog box, click the Web tab, as shown in Figure 12-14. In the Web Pages area, select the My Current Home Page item.

3. Alternatively, you can click the New button to select another Web page to display on your desktop. The New Desktop Item dialog box appears, as shown in Figure 12-15, offering the following options:

- Click the Visit Gallery button to open a Microsoft Internet Explorer Desktop Gallery site. Here you find Investor Ticker, CBS SportsLine, Weather Map from MSNBC, and more. Just click the Add to Active Desktop button to add each item.

- Enter the URL of a Web page that you'd like to display on your desktop in the Location text box.

- Click the Browse button to locate an HTML document or picture to place on your desktop. This opens your Internet Explorer Favorites folder, where you can select a favorite site and click OK to specify it.

4. To save your new Active Desktop settings, click OK.

 With several types of online connections providing an always-on connection mode (such as cable), you might find that rather than using Active Desktop, you can just as easily keep your browser open to the page that you want to view and choose View↷Refresh every now and then. This diverts less of your computer's resources to keeping online information constantly refreshed.

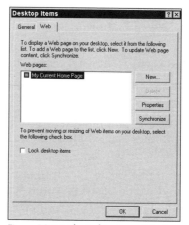

Figure 12-14: The Desktop Items dialog box, Web tab

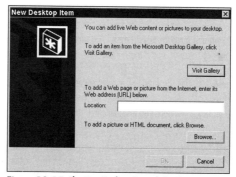

Figure 12-15: The New Desktop Item dialog box

Set Up a Screen Saver

1. Right-click the desktop and choose Properties. Click the Screen Saver tab to display it, as shown in Figure 12-16.

2. From the Screen Saver drop-down list, select a screen saver.

3. Use the arrows in the Wait *xx* Minutes text box to set the number of inactivity minutes that Windows XP waits before displaying the screen saver.

4. Click the Preview button (see Figure 12-17) to take a peek at your screen saver of choice. When you're happy with your settings, click OK.

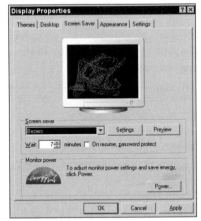

Figure 12-16: The Display Properties dialog box, Screen Saver tab

 Screen savers used to be required to keep your monitor from burning out because an image was held on your screen for too long. Newer monitors don't require this, but people are attached to their screen savers, so the feature persists. Screen savers are also useful for hiding what's on your screen from curious passersby if you happen to wander away from your desk for a while. If you want a more personalized screen saver experience than the rotating Windows logos provide, choose the My Pictures Slideshow from the list of screensavers. This displays the images saved in your My Pictures folder, one after another. Just make sure that you don't have anything in that folder that you'd rather keep private!

 Some screen savers allow you to modify their settings: for example, how fast they display or how many lines they draw onscreen. To customize this, click the Settings button when in the Display Properties dialog box on the Screen Saver tab.

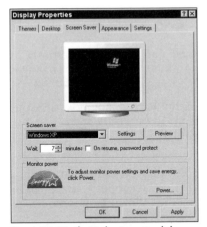

Figure 12-17: The Bezier screen saver

Change the Windows XP Color Scheme

1. Right-click the desktop and choose Properties.

2. In the resulting Display Properties dialog box, click the Appearance tab display it, as shown in Figure 12-18.

3. Select a color scheme from the Color Scheme drop-down list.

4. To customize the selected preset color scheme, click the Advanced button.

5. In the resulting Advanced Appearance dialog box, as shown in Figure 12-19, select items one by one from the Item drop-down list. Make changes you wish using the Size, Color, and Font settings.

6. Click OK to accept the advanced settings, and then click OK to close the Display Properties dialog box and apply all changes.

 When customizing a color scheme, be aware that not all screen elements allow you to modify all settings. For example, setting an Application Background doesn't make the Font setting available — because it's just a background setting. Makes sense, huh?

 Some colors are easier on the eyes than others. For example green is more restful to look at than orange. Choose a color scheme that is pleasant to look at and easy on the eyes!

Figure 12-18: The Display Properties dialog box, Appearance tab

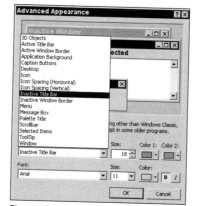

Figure 12-19: The Advanced Appearance dialog box

Working with Sound

Who doesn't love to hear music? It soothes the savage breast and gets us dancing and singing. To spice up the sometimes-tedious time you spend working on your PC, add a dash of music! You can play music — or for that matter, any kind of audio file — from your computer and forget the CD player.

Your computer can play, record, and download music as well as tap into radio stations with ease. With a sound card installed and speakers attached, you have a hi-tech desktop boombox. By using Windows XP media programs, you can create playlists and even listen to your favorite radio station while working or playing on your desktop or laptop PC.

When you feel the need for sound, here's what your PC lets you do:

➡ Set up your sound card and adjust speaker and volume settings.

➡ Set up your Windows XP sound scheme.

➡ Download and play audio files.

➡ Copy music to a CD or DVD, play music with Windows Media Player, and record music with Windows Sound Recorder.

Chapter 13

Get ready to . . .

Set Up a Sound Card

1. Choose Start➪Control Panel➪Sounds, Speech, and Audio Devices, and then click the Sounds and Audio Devices link.

2. In the resulting Sounds and Audio Devices dialog box, which opens with the Volume tab sheet displayed, click the Hardware tab to modify sound devices.

3. Click the sound card that you want to modify and then click the Properties button.

4. In the resulting Audio Device Properties dialog box, as shown in Figure 13-1, click the arrow on the Device Usage drop-down list and choose the Use This Device (Enable) setting if it isn't already selected.

5. If you want to make sure you have the most current driver, click the Driver tab (see Figure 13-2) and then click the Update Driver button.

6. When you're done making settings, click OK.

 Read your user's manual before doing this procedure. Some sound cards are built into the motherboard, but others require that you take some steps to disable the old card before installing the new.

 The Sound Troubleshooter, which you can access from the Hardware tab of the Sounds and Audio Devices dialog box, takes you through testing your sound card step by step and isolating various problems. But remember the basics: You have to have speakers connected to your computer, and the volume setting on your computer can't be muted. If you neglect to properly set either of these two vital requirements, don't be ashamed — just about everyone has done it, myself included!

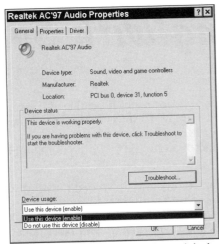

Figure 13-1: The Sounds and Audio Devices dialog box, Hardware tab

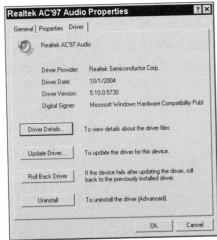

Figure 13-2: The Audio Device Properties dialog box, Driver tab

Set Up Speakers

1. Attach speakers to your computer by plugging them into the appropriate connection (often labeled with a little megaphone or speaker symbol) on your PC, laptop, or monitor.

2. Choose Start⇨Control Panel⇨Sounds, Speech, and Audio Devices, and then click the Change the Speaker Settings link.

3. In the resulting Sounds and Audio Devices Properties dialog box (see Figure 13-3), click the Volume tab; under Speaker Settings, click the Advanced button. (*Note:* The Volume tab should be selected by default; if it's not, click to display it.)

4. In the resulting Advanced Audio Properties dialog box, as shown in Figure 13-4, use the Speaker Setup drop-down list to choose the best option for your computer; then click Apply.

5. Click the Performance tab of the Advanced Audio Properties dialog box to display it. Click either of two sliders to modify these settings:

   • **Hardware acceleration:** A higher setting can help your PC by taking some sound processing chores off its plate. Changing this setting might help with some typical glitches that can occur. (The glitches mostly occur when playing games, which drains your system resources as they deal with high-quality graphics and sound playback at the same time.)

   • **Sample rate conversion quality:** A setting for sound quality. If you're experiencing problems with audio crashing your system or slowing your system's performance, putting this at a lower setting might help.

6. Click OK to save the new settings.

Figure 13-3: The Sounds and Audio Devices Properties dialog box

 If you're an audio pro and have a professional-quality sound device (such as an audio mixer) connected to your computer, the No Speaker setting is most appropriate one to select in the Speaker Setup drop-down list.

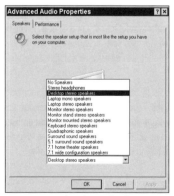

Figure 13-4: The Advanced Audio Properties dialog box

Configure Audio Volume

1. Choose Start⇨Control Panel⇨Sounds, Speech, and Audio Devices, and then click the Adjust System Volume link to display the Sounds and Audio Devices Properties dialog box, as shown in Figure 13-5.

2. Under the Device Volume section, click the Advanced button to open the Volume Control dialog box, as shown in Figure 13-6. Make any of the following settings:

   • **Volume sliders:** Move these to adjust the volume up and down.

   • **Balance slider:** If you have a stereo device, use this slider to adjust sound between right and left speakers.

   • **Mute All** or **Mute check box:** To mute all devices or the selected device, select the Mute All or Mute check box underneath the specific device, respectively.

3. Click the Close button, and then click OK to close the Sounds and Audio Devices Properties dialog box.

 The Master Volume control works for all sound devices. If you have other devices installed (for example, a synthesizer or CD player), you can use individual sliders to adjust their volumes separately.

 A handy shortcut exists for adjusting the volume of your default sound devices. Click the Volume button (which looks like a little gray speaker) on the right side of the Windows XP taskbar. Use the slider on the Volume pop-up that appears to adjust the volume, or select the Mute check box to turn sounds off temporarily.

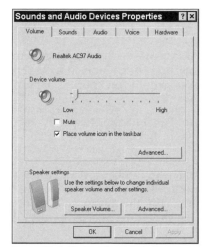

Figure 13-5: The Sounds and Audio Devices Properties dialog box, Volume tab

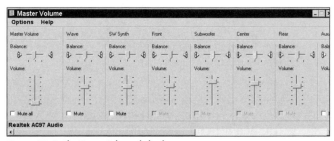

Figure 13-6: The Master Volume dialog box

Adjust Your Sound Scheme

1. Choose Start⇨Control Panel⇨Sounds, Speech, and Audio Devices.

2. In the resulting Sounds, Speech, and Audio Devices window, as shown in Figure 13-7, click Change the Sound Scheme link.

3. In the Sounds and Audio Devices dialog box that appears, click to display the Sounds tab, if it's not already displayed (see Figure 13-8).

4. Click to display the Sound Scheme drop-down list and choose the sound scheme you prefer:

   • **Windows Default** uses the sound scheme that came installed with Windows XP.

   • **No Sounds** turns off all sounds associated with Windows events.

5. Click OK to save the new settings.

 If you wish to change individual sounds associated with Windows events, such as exiting Windows, you can click an individual event in the Program Events list and then choose a new setting from the Sounds drop-down list. You can also click Browse to display the Browse for Device and Connect Sound dialog box. When you finish, click the Save As button to save the new Sound Scheme.

Figure 13-7: The Sounds, Speech, and Audio Devices window

Figure 13-8: The Sounds and Audio Devices Properties dialog box, Sound tab

Download a Sound File

1. Depending on how the Web site you're visiting has set things up, you do one of the following:

   - Click a download button or link and follow the instructions for selecting a destination location on your hard drive to download the file to.

   - Right-click the sound file link and choose Save Target As. In the Save As dialog box that appears, use the Save In drop-down list to locate a place to save the file, enter a File Name, and click Save. A dialog box (see Figure 13-9) shows the download progress; when it's completed, click the Open button. A player that the sound file is associated with, such as MusicMatch Jukebox or Windows Media Player, opens and plays the file.

   - Click the sound file link, and a download dialog box opens. Follow the steps in the previous option to select a download location, name the file, and proceed with the download.

2. When the file finishes downloading, it might open and play automatically in a media player, such as Windows Media Player, as shown in Figure 13-10. If it doesn't, you have to take one of the following actions:

   - You can locate the saved file by using Windows Explorer; then double-click the file to play it.

   - One final option is to open Windows Media Player, choose File➪Open, locate the file, and open it. Then use the player's tools to play the file.

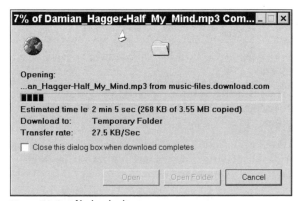

Figure 13-9: A file download in progress

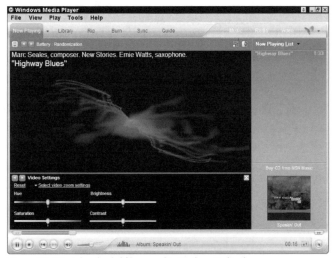

Figure 13-10: A downloaded file opened in Windows Media Player

Create a Playlist

1. Choose Start➪All Programs➪Accessories➪Entertainment➪ Windows Media Player.

2. Click the Library tab. On the File menu choose New Now Playing List.

3. Click an item in either pane of the Library, and drag it to the area on the far right labelled "Drag items here to build a list of items to play" (see Figure 13-11).

4. Click the Add to Library button (see Figure 13-12) and choose Add Currently Playing Playlist. In the Save As dialog box that appears enter a name in the File Name field and click Save.

5. The playlist now appears under My Playlists in the left pane. Click the playlist. All titles in the playlist appear in the list on the right. Now you can double-click any item in the playlist to play it.

 You can rename or delete a playlist. Right-click the list under the My Playlists category in the left pane of the Media Library and then choose Rename or Delete, respectively.

 You can also create a new playlist by right-clicking either the My Playlists or Auto Playlists item in the left pane of the Library tab and choosing New.

Figure 13-11: A new blank playlist

Figure 13-12: Saving a playlist

Copy Music to a CD or DVD

1. Insert a blank CD suitable for storing audio files in your computer CD-RW drive. (If you have a DVD player, follow these same steps by using your DVD drive.)

2. Open the Windows Media Player, click the Burn tab.

3. Click the arrow to display the list of music on your computer and choose one; its contents appear in the left pane.

4. Make sure the appropriate drive is showing in the right-hand pane; if it's not, click the arrow to the right of that field and select a location for your CD-RW or DVD.

5. Click in the check boxes to select the items you want to burn, and then click Start Burn (see Figure 13-13). Windows Media Player begins to copy your playlist onto your storage disc.

When you copy music to a CD, you create an exact copy. However, if you copy music from a CD onto your computer, Windows Media Player automatically compresses it. That's because music files are big and can fill up your hard drive fast. Compressed music files lose some sound quality, but given the quality of your computer's speakers you probably won't notice the difference.

Want to copy music from a CD or DVD into your Windows Media Player Library? Just put the disc in your computer drive and click the Copy from CD button on the left. When the list of titles on the CD appears, click to select the ones you want, and then click the Copy Music button in the top-right corner.

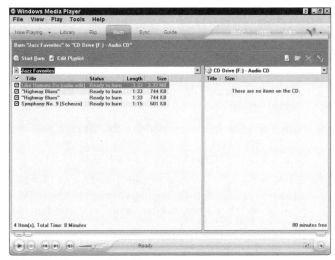

Figure 13-13: Copy music to a CD

You can add a playlist to your burn list by right-clicking it in the left pane of the library tab and choosing Add to Burn List.

Play Music with Windows Media Player

1. Choose Start⇨All Programs⇨Accessories⇨Entertainment⇨ Windows Media Player.

2. Click the Library tab near the top of the window to display the library, as shown in Figure 13-14. Click an item in the left pane to open it; the titles of the songs are displayed in the right pane.

3. Use the buttons here to do the following:

   • Click a track and then click the **Play** button to play it.

   • Click the **Stop** button to stop playback.

   • Click the **Next** or **Previous** buttons to move to the next or previous track in an album or playlist.

   • Use the **Mute** and **Volume** controls to pump the sound up or down without having to modify the Windows XP volume settings.

 Note that different *skins* display controls that have a different look. Choose View⇨Skin Chooser to see the available skins you can apply the player. When you see a skin you like, click Apply Skin. You can also download additional skins from Microsoft by choosing Help⇨Windows Media Player Online.

Figure 13-14: The Windows Media Player Library

 Skins may make your controls look so different you're not sure how to use them. However, don't despair. Until you get used to the new controls, just hover your mouse over each control and a ToolTip appears telling you which is which.

Listen to Online Radio

1. With Windows Media Player open, click the Radio tab. The MSN Radio page appears (see Figure 13-15).

2. Click on a featured station or click on a + sign next to an item to display lists such as Fan Favorites, Local Sounds, or on a category of music such as Jazz to locate a station. Click the plus sign to the left of categories to display the options under it (see Figure 3-16).

3. Click on the station you want to listen to; the station plays. You can use the controls at the bottom left of the screen to stop, pause, play, or move forward or backward in the radio programming.

4. When you are done listening, click Radio again to return to MSN Radio, or click Music to leave MSN Radio and return to the main Windows Media Explorer interface.

 Some radio stations require that you pay for a subscription so it will cost you to get your music. One cue to a station that asks that you pay are the words "Try it free today," which suggests that tomorrow it may not be!

 If you need to stop the music from playing you have a few options. You can click the Stop button to stop it; if you do this you have to restart the station, which goes back to the songs you've already heard. You can click Pause, which pauses the playback where you stop and then resumes where you left off. You can click the Mute button to silence the playback; when you click Mute again the music will have moved on for as long as you muted it.

Figure 13-15: Use the Radio tab of Windows Media Player to access online radio stations

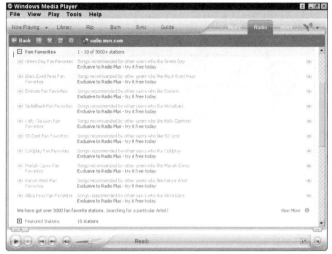

Figure 13-16: The MSN Radio page

Record with Windows Sound Recorder

1. Attach a microphone to your computer. (See your computer manual for how to do this.)

2. Choose Start➪All Programs➪Accessories➪Entertainment➪ Sound Recorder.

3. In the resulting Sound Recorder window (see Figure 13-17), click the circular Record button.

4. The Position and Length boxes begin to record the number of seconds of your recording, and the slider begins to move to the right. Click the rectangular Stop button shown in Figure 13-18 to stop the recording.

5. To play back the recording, click the triangular Play button. Click Stop to stop the playback at any time.

6. Choose File➪Save and use the resulting Save As dialog box to save the recording.

7. Click Close to close the Sound Recorder window.

 While playing back a recording, you can rewind or fast forward either by clicking and dragging the slider bar backward or forward, or by clicking the Rewind button (two left-facing arrows) or the Forward button (two right-facing arrows).

 You can add various special effects to your recording by using the commands in the Effects menu. For example, you can speed up or slow down the recording, add an echo, or play it in reverse.

Figure 13-17: The Sound Recorder window ready to record

Figure 13-18: A recording in progress

Working with Digital Imaging and Video

Camcorders and digital cameras have become as ubiquitous as popcorn at your local movie theater. Your PC gives you the tools to play and edit movies to your heart's content and manipulate digital images. Microsoft has built tools into Windows XP to make this possible, including Movie Maker for editing and organizing movies, Media Player to play movies, Windows Picture and Fax Viewer for viewing and editing photos and Scanner and Camera Wizard for getting photos from your...you guessed it...scanner or camera!

You can use sample movie clips included with Windows XP in the My Videos folder or photos in the My Pictures folder to get you started. You can also upload video files from your camcorder and photos from your digital camera, or download movies or photos from the Internet.

When you have movies and photos to play with, here's what you can do:

- ⇒ Play back your movies using features to play, pause, stop, fast-forward, or rewind.
- ⇒ Open movies in Movie Maker and play with video effects.
- ⇒ Upload, view, edit, and print photos.
- ⇒ Scan images with the Windows Scanner and Camera Wizard.

Play Movies with Windows Media Player

1. Choose Start➪All Programs➪Accessories➪Entertainment➪ Windows Media Player.

2. Click the Maximize button in the resulting Media Player window. If the Video Settings are not displayed, choose View➪Enhancements➪Video Settings.

3. In the Video Settings displayed at the bottom of the player, click and drag any of the following sliders (as shown in Figure 14-1) to adjust the settings:

   - **Hue:** Relates to where a color falls on the color spectrum (green to blue, for example)

   - **Brightness:** How light or dark the image is

   - **Saturation:** How pure a color's hue is, from gray to pure color

   - **Contrast:** The variation between dark and light colors

4. Choose File➪Open to display the Open dialog box.

5. Use the Look In field to locate the folder that contains the file you want to play. Click the file and then click Open. The movie opens in Media Player.

6. Click the Play button in the bottom-left corner to begin the playback (see Figure 14-2). Adjust the volume of any sound track by using the Mute or Volume tools.

7. Click the Close button to close Media Player.

 To stop the movie before it finishes, click the Stop button. Note that the Previous and Next tools aren't available for single movie clips — they jump you from one track to another when playing sound files.

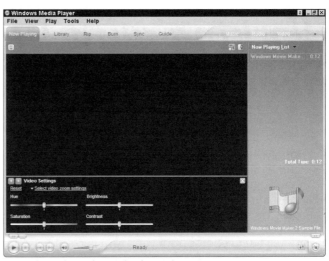

Figure 14-1: The Windows Media Player video settings

Figure 14-2: A movie in playback mode

Create a New Project in Windows Movie Maker

1. Choose Start⇨All Programs⇨Accessories⇨Entertainment⇨ Windows Movie Maker to open the Movie Maker window.

2. Choose File⇨New Project to open a new blank Movie Maker file.

3. Choose File⇨Import Into Collections to open the Import File dialog box.

4. Use the Look In drop-down list to locate the folder where the movie file you want to open is saved.

5. Click the file and then click Open to open the file in the Movie Maker window, as shown in Figure 14-3. (**Note:** You can repeat this procedure to open more than one movie file in a project.)

6. Click clips displayed in the Collection pane and drag them down to the storyboard along the bottom of the window, as shown in Figure 14-4.

7. Choose File⇨Save Project. In the Save Project As dialog box, enter a filename in the File Name text box and then click Save.

 After you create a project, what can you actually do with it? When you've created a project and imported movies into it, you can use various features of Movie Maker to edit, reorganize, and playback movies. With more than one movie imported into a project, for example, you could pick and choose clips from each of them and organize them to create your own unique movie.

 Another nice feature when playing back movies in Windows Movie Maker is the ability to view movies with the full screen by clicking the Full Screen button. Press Esc to exit Full Screen mode.

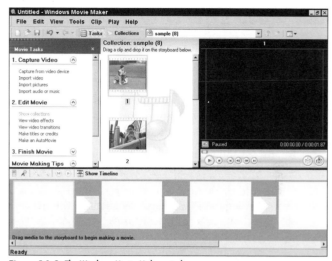

Figure 14-3: The Windows Movie Maker window

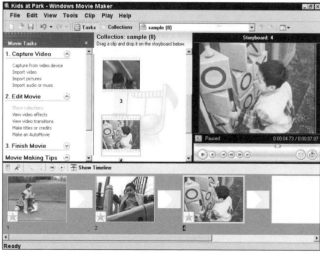

Figure 14-4: Movie clips on the storyboard

Add Video Effects to a Movie

1. With a movie open in Movie Maker, choose Tools⇨ Video Effects.

2. In the Video Effects pane, as shown in Figure 14-5, click an effect and drag it to a clip in your movie on the storyboard or timeline. A star appears on a clip to indicate that it has an effect applied.

3. To add several effects to a selected clip at once, choose Clip⇨Video⇨Video Effects.

4. In the Add or Remove Video Effects dialog box, as shown in Figure 14-6, click any effect in the list on the left and then click Add. To remove an effect, click any effect in the list on the right and then click Remove.

5. When you're finished, click OK. When you click the Play button to play the video, you can view your stunning effects.

 Note that some of the effects are available only if you purchase Microsoft Plus! If you select one of those effects, a window pops up informing you of this and providing a link to a Web site where you can purchase this software to download or ship to you for about $20. Microsoft Plus! includes various media-enhancing tools and clips.

Figure 14-5: The Video Effects pane

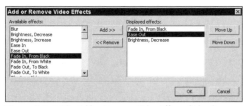

Figure 14-6: The Add or Remove Video Effects dialog box

Install an Imaging Device

1. Connect your imaging device (such as a digital camera) to your PC; you might need to plug a connector to a USB port or insert a removable memory card into a card reader, depending on your device and model.

2. Typically, your PC automatically detects the device and the Found New Hardware pop-up appears. Windows XP will automatically set the hardware up using Windows-included drivers and redisplay pop-up letting you know the device was set up.

3. If your PC doesn't automatically detect the device, choose Start⇨Control Panel⇨Printers and Other Hardware.

4. Click the Scanners and Cameras link.

5. In the Scanners and Cameras window that appears (see Figure 14-7), click Add an Imaging Device in the Imaging Tasks panel.

6. In the Scanner and Camera Installation Wizard window that appears, click Next.

7. In the following wizard screen (see Figure 14-8), click the manufacturer of your device in the Manufacturer list and then the device model in the Model list. Click Next.

8. On the next wizard screen, choose the port to which you've attached the device and then click Next. On the following screen, type a name for the device and then click Next.

9. On the final wizard screen, click Finish to complete the set up.

 If your model isn't listed in the wizard Manufacturer list, insert the disk/c that came with your device and click the Have Disk button to install a driver.

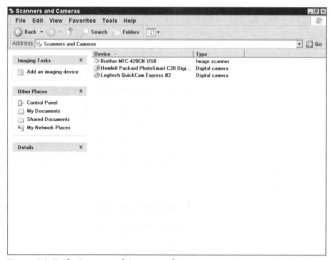

Figure 14-7: The Scanner and Camera window

 Some digital cameras shut off automatically after a certain period of time of inactivity. If you have trouble getting your PC to detect your camera, make sure that the camera has not shut itself off.

Figure 14-8: The Microsoft Scanner and Camera Installation Wizard

View a Digital Image in Windows Picture and Fax Viewer

1. Locate an image file on your hard drive, network, or storage media by using Windows Explorer. (Choose Start⇨All Programs⇨Accessories⇨Windows Explorer.)

2. Right-click the filename or icon and choose Open With⇨Windows Picture and Fax Viewer. In the resulting Windows Picture and Fax Viewer, as shown in Figure 14-9, you can use the tools at the bottom to do any of the following:

   • The **Previous Image** and **Next Image** icons move to a previous or following image, respectively, in the same folder.

   • The **Best Fit** and **Actual Size** icons modify the display of the image in the Picture and Fax Viewer.

   • The **Start Slide Show** icon begins a full-screen slide show of images.

   • The **Zoom In** and **Zoom Out** icons enlarge or shrink, respectively, the image display.

   • The **Rotate Clockwise** and **Rotate Counterclockwise** icons spin the image 90 degrees at a time (see Figure 14-10).

   • **Delete, Print, Copy To,** and **Close All** do just what their names say.

3. When you've finished viewing images, click the Close button in the top right-hand corner to close the Viewer.

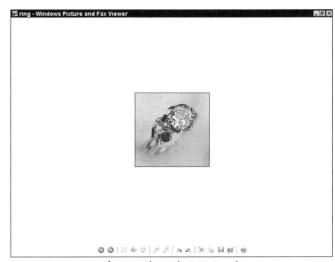

Figure 14-9: A picture of a ring in the Windows Picture and Fax Viewer

Figure 14-10: A rotated image

Print a Photo with Photo Printing Wizard

1. Locate a file using Windows Explorer or by opening your My Pictures folder (choose Start⇨My Pictures) if it is stored there.

2. Right-click the photo and then choose Print.

3. In the resulting Photo Printing Wizard window, click Next.

4. In the Picture Selection window that appears (see Figure 14-11), select the check box for any picture you want to print; then click Next. *Note:* This window appears only if you have more than one photo in the folder.

5. In the resulting Printing Options window (see Figure 14-12), click the What Printer Do You Want to Use drop-down list arrow and then choose the printer you want from the list that appears.

6. To change print settings, click the Printing Preferences button and make changes in the Properties dialog box that appears. Click OK to save any changes and then click Next.

7. In the resulting Layout Selection window, click a layout in the list and then click Next. The photo prints, and the final wizard window appears. Click Finish to close the wizard.

 If you choose a layout that allows multiple images on a single page, you can use the Number of Times to Use Each Picture setting on the Layout Selection window to control how many times the picture prints on a page.

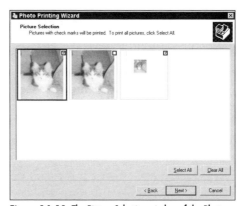

Figure 14-11: The Picture Selection window of the Photo Printing Wizard

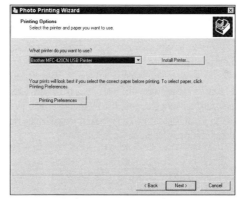

Figure 14-12: The Printing Options window

Save a Photo in Another Format

1. Choose Start⇨My Pictures (or use Windows Explorer to locate a photo saved to another folder).

2. In the resulting My Pictures folder, right-click the photo and choose Open.

3. In the Windows Picture and Fax Viewer that opens (see Figure 14-13), click the Copy To button (it looks like a small floppy disk).

4. In the Copy to dialog box that appears (see Figure 14-14), click the Save as Type drop-down list arrow and choose another format to save to from the list that appears.

5. If you want to rename the file, type a new name in the File Name field.

6. Click Save. The file is saved in the new format.

 Various graphics formats offer different advantages. For example, JPEG compresses an image to a more compact size that's useful for e-mailing or when creating Web sites; however, this compression can cause a loss of image quality. TIFF and bitmap are compatible with a great many software programs; TIFF retains quality at a slightly smaller size than bitmaps. PNG is the newest format on the block, developed specifically for use on the Web.

Figure 14-13: The Windows Picture and Fax Viewer

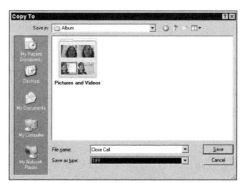

Figure 14-14: The Copy To dialog box

Use the Windows Scanner and Camera Wizard

1. Place a page, a picture, or some other object (like those cool sports decals you've been collecting) in your scanner.

2. Choose Start⇨All Programs⇨Accessories⇨Scanner and Camera Wizard. If the Select Device dialog box appears, click your scanner and then choose OK. If this dialog box doesn't appear proceed to Step 3.

3. On the first Scanner and Camera wizard screen that appears, click Next. In the next screen (see Figure 14-15), choose your preferences for scanning by selecting one of these radio buttons: Color Picture, Grayscale Picture, Black and White Picture or Text, or Custom. Click Next.

4. In the resulting Scanner and Camera Wizard screen (see Figure 14-16), designate information about the file and then click Next:

   • In the first drop-down list, enter a name for a group of pictures or select a group that you've already created.

   • In the second drop-down list, select a format for the file, such as BMP (bitmap) or JPEG.

   • In the third drop-down list, enter a location to store the file.

5. On the resulting Scanning Picture screen, you see the progress of the scan. Sit tight or go grab a slice of pizza while your scanner and computer do their thing.

6. When the scanning is complete, a dialog box appears offering three options; choose one, and follow any one of these options to complete working with your pictures:

   • Publish these pictures to a Web site.

   • Order prints of these pictures from a photo-printing Web site.

   • Nothing. I'm finished working with these pictures.

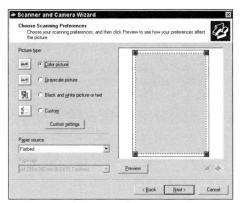

Figure 14-15: The Scanner and Camera Wizard

 If you choose Custom in Step 3, click the Custom Settings button if you want to monkey around with things like resolution. For most documents, however, one of the first three settings will do just fine.

Figure 14-16: Specifying name, format, and location for your file

Part IV
Going Online

The 5th Wave   By Rich Tennant

©RICHTENNANT

"I guess you could say this is the hub of our network."

Accessing the Internet

*T*he Internet has become a way of life for most of us. It's the way people communicate, transfer files, share images and music, shop for just about everything, and research topics from Antarctica to Zeus.

Getting connected to the Internet is easy to do. Most Internet service providers (ISPs) supply software to set up your connection automatically. But you can connect in a few different ways, and you'll encounter a few different technologies along the way. You might also need to tinker around with some settings in Windows XP to get things working just the way you want them to.

In this chapter, you find out how to make and manage Internet connections, including:

- ➡ **Setting up your connection:** A New Connection Wizard helps you with this process. You can specify your default connection to control how you log on to the Internet.

- ➡ **Modifying settings:** Whether you use a TCP/IP or an always-on connection (such as cable or DSL), you discover the ins and outs of configuring them as well as how to share your Internet connection with someone else.

- ➡ **Using your Internet connection to connect to a network:** If you're like many people, you might need to tap into your workplace network from a remote location. It's easy to do, and you can read all about it in this chapter.

Chapter
15

Get ready to . . .

Set Up a New ISP Internet Connection

1. Choose Start⇨My Network Places.

2. In the resulting window, click the View Network Connections link.

3. In the resulting Network Connections window (see Figure 15-1), click the Create a New Connection link in the Network Tasks pane.

4. In the New Connection Wizard dialog box, click Next.

5. In the resulting dialog box, accept the default selection of Connect to the Internet and then click Next.

6. In the resulting New Connection Wizard, as shown in Figure 15-2, select one of the following three options to set up a new ISP account:

   • The **Choose from a List of Internet Service Providers (ISPs)** option allows you to quickly set up MSN or choose from a list of other ISPs. Making this choice leads you to the Internet Connection Wizard, where your choices vary depending on the service provider you select.

   • If you have all the information about your ISP account and want to enter it manually, **Set Up My Connection Manually** is the choice for you.

   • The **Use the CD I Got from an ISP** option is pretty obvious. If you have a CD, whether an ISP sent it to you or you picked it up at a store, select this option to activate the setup instructions for that ISP.

7. Click Next and follow the instructions to finish setting up your ISP connection. *Note:* You need to select the type of connection (for example, cable modem or dialup) and create a user name and password for your new account during this process.

Figure 15-1: The Network Connections window

In many cases, if you have a disc from your ISP, you don't need to follow the steps above at all. Just pop that CD into your CD-ROM drive, and in no time, a window appears and gives you instructions for setting up your account.

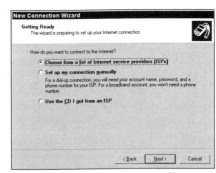

Figure 15-2: The New Connection Wizard, Getting Ready dialog box

Set Up a Dial-Up Connection to an Existing ISP Account Manually

1. Choose Start⇨My Network Places.

2. In the resulting My Network Places window, click the View Network Connections link.

3. In the Network Connections window under Network Tasks, click the Create a New Connection link.

4. In the New Connection Wizard dialog box, click Next.

5. In the resulting dialog box, accept the default selection of Connect to the Internet and then click Next.

6. In the resulting dialog box, select the Set Up My Connection Manually option and then click Next.

7. In the Internet Connection dialog box, as shown in Figure 15-3, select the Connect Using a Dial-up Modem option.

8. In the next two dialog boxes, enter your ISP name and then the phone number used to connect.

9. In the Internet Account Information (see Figure 15-4), enter the following information:

   • Your user name and password

   • Whether this is the default Internet connection

   • Whether to automatically use this name and password for this connection from this computer

10. When the final wizard dialog box appears, click Finish to create the connection.

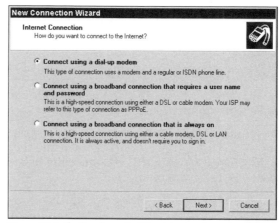

Figure 15-3: The New Connection Wizard, Internet Connection dialog box

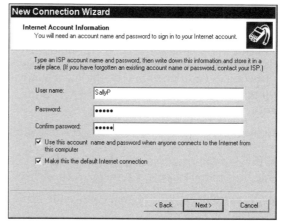

Figure 15-4: New Connection Wizard, Internet Account Information dialog boxes

Share an Internet Connection on a Network

1. Choose Start➪My Network Places.

2. In the resulting My Network Places window, click the View Network Connections link.

3. In the resulting Network Connections window (see Figure 15-5), click a connection to select it and then click the Change Settings of This Connection link in the Network Tasks area on the left.

4. In the resulting Properties dialog box (the name of the dialog box varies based on the name of your Internet service provider), click the Advanced tab.

5. Select the Allow Other Network Users to Connect through This Computer's Internet Connection check box (see Figure 15-6).

6. If you want to dial this connection automatically when another computer on your network tries to access it, select the Establish a Dial-up Connection Whenever a Computer on My Network Attempts to Access the Internet check box.

7. If you want other people on your network to control the shared Internet connection by enabling or disabling it, select the Allow Other Network Users to Control or Disable the Shared Internet Connection check box.

8. Click OK twice to save the shared connection settings.

 Users on your network also have to make some settings to use your shared connection. They have to configure TCP/IP (Transmission Control Protocol/Internet Protocol) settings on their local area connections so that they get an IP connection automatically.

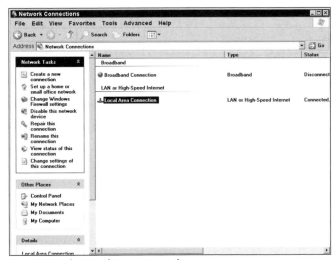

Figure 15-5: The Network Connections window

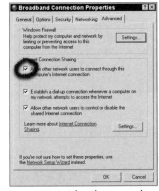

Figure 15-6: Selected options in the Properties dialog box

Configure a TCP/IP Connection

1. Choose Start⇨My Network Places.

2. In the resulting My Network Places window, click the View Network Connections link.

3. Click the connection that you want to set up and then click Change Settings of this Connection.

4. In the resulting Properties dialog box (the name of the dialog box varies based on the name of your Internet service provider) display the Networking tab (see Figure 15-7).

5. On the Networking tab, in the This Connection Uses the Following Items area, select the Internet Protocol (TCP/IP) option, and then click the Properties button.

6. In the Internet Protocol (TCP/IP) Properties dialog box that appears, as shown in Figure 15-8, select the Obtain an IP Address Automatically option and Obtain DNS Server Address Automatically to allow addresses to be assigned automatically. Then click OK twice.

 Although you can enter addresses manually in the Internet Protocol (TCP/IP) Properties dialog box, I recommend letting them be assigned automatically. Then if there's a change in your setup, you don't have to go in and manually modify addresses. This also saves you the hassle of having to manually configure certain settings, such as the Domain Name Service, which implements the Domain Name System (DNS). If you don't want to worry about such techie things (and who does?), just let addresses be assigned automatically.

 TCP stands for Transmission Control Protocol. This is a set of standards for how data messages are broken down into packages to be sent across the Internet using IP, or Internet Protocol.

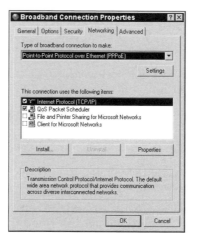

Figure 15-7: The Properties dialog box, Networking tab

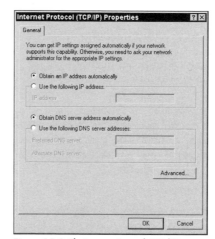

Figure 15-8: The Internet Protocol (TCP/IP) Properties dialog box, General tab

Set Up an Always-On Connection

1. Choose Start⇨My Network Places.

2. In the resulting My Network Places window, click the View Network Connections link.

3. In the Network Connections window under Network Tasks, click the Create a New Connection link.

4. In the New Connection Wizard dialog box, click Next.

5. In the resulting dialog box, accept the default selection of Connect to the Internet and then click Next.

6. In the Getting Ready dialog box, as shown in Figure 15-9, select the Set Up My Connection Manually option and then click Next.

7. In the Internet Connection dialog box, as shown in Figure 15-10, select the Connect Using a Broadband Connection that Is Always On option and then click Next.

8. In the following dialog boxes, the wizard notifies you that Windows XP will detect your connection and make settings for you. When you reach the final wizard dialog box, click Finish to complete the process.

 You might not have to do any of the above steps to set up an always-on connection. If your provider doesn't require a user name and password to be entered, simply connect your broadband or cable modem and then restart your computer. Windows XP should automatically detect the connection.

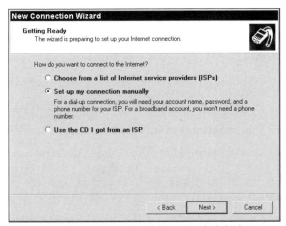

Figure 15-9: New Connection Wizard, Getting Ready dialog box

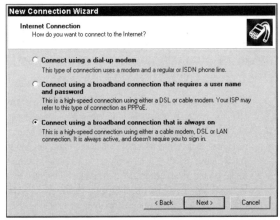

Figure 15-10: New Connection Wizard, Internet Connection dialog box

Set Up a Connection to the Network at Your Workplace

1. Choose Start⇨My Network Places.

2. In the resulting My Network Places window, click the View Network Connections link.

3. In the Network Connections window under Network Tasks, click the Create a New Connection link.

4. In the New Connection Wizard dialog box, click Next.

5. In the Network Connection Type dialog box shown in Figure 15-11, click the Connect to the Network at My Workplace radio button and then click Next.

6. In the resulting dialog box, choose either the Dial-Up Connection or Virtual Private Network Connection option, and then click Next.

7. In the next two dialog boxes, enter a name of your choosing for the connection such as "Home Network" and then choose one of the following:

   - **For a dial-up connection:** Enter a phone number. (See Figure 15-12.)

   - **For a VPN connection:** Select whether or not to automatically dial the initial connection. If you choose not to dial automatically, you have to initiate the dialing yourself by right-clicking the connection name in the Network Connections window and choosing Connect.

8. When you reach the final wizard dialog box, click Finish to complete the wizard.

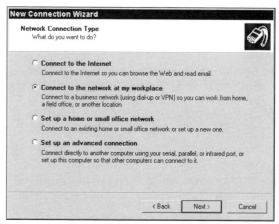

Figure 15-11: The Network Connection Type dialog box

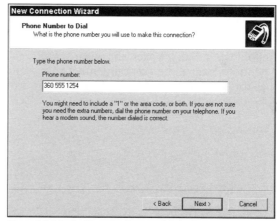

Figure 15-12: The Phone Number to Dial dialog box

Designate Your Default Connection

1. Choose Start➪Control Panel.

2. In the Control Panel window (assuming you are using the Windows XP default Category view and not the Classic view), click the Network and Internet Connections link. In the resulting window (see Figure 15-13), click the Set Up or Change Your Internet Connection link.

3. In the resulting Internet Properties dialog box (see Figure 15-14), with the Connections tab displayed, click the connection that you want to make the default.

4. Click the Set Default button and then click OK.

 Your computer uses the default connection anytime you click a link or open your browser. However, you can still manually open any connection by opening the Network Connections window, right-clicking any connection, and choosing Connect.

 If your default connection is through an external modem and you're having trouble getting online, check the obvious: Loose or incorrect connections to your modem can stop you from getting online.

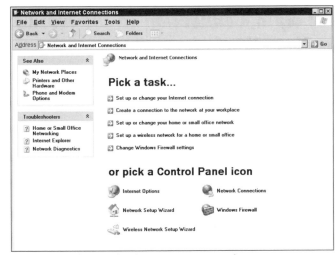

Figure 15-13: The Network and Internet Connections window

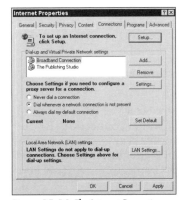

Figure 15-14: The Internet Properties dialog box, Connections tab

Remove an Internet Connection

1. Choose Start➪Control Panel.

2. In the Control Panel window, click the Network and Internet Connections link.

3. In the Network and Internet Connections window (refer to Figure 15-13), click the Set Up or Change Your Internet Connection link.

4. In the resulting Internet Properties dialog box (see Figure 15-15), with the Connections tab displayed, click the connection that you want to delete and then click the Remove button.

5. Click OK.

Repair a Connection

1. Choose Start➪My Network Places.

2. In the My Network Places window, click the View Network Connections link.

3. In the Network Connections window (see Figure 15-16), right-click the connection and then choose Repair from the shortcut menu.

 Sometimes repairing a connection doesn't do the trick. In that case, it's best to delete the connection and just create it again by clicking the Create a New Connection link in the Network Connections window and then entering the correct settings.

Figure 15-15: The Internet Properties dialog box

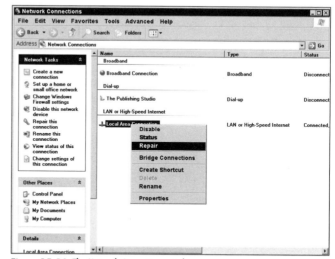

Figure 15-16: The Network Connections window

Browsing the Web with Internet Explorer

To drive around the Internet superhighway, you need a good vehicle. A *browser* is a program that you can use to get around the Internet, and Internet Explorer (IE) is one of the best.

IE is built into Windows XP — it's also made by Microsoft, so it offers familiar functionality to Windows XP users. This is good news for you because using IE allows you to:

➡ **Navigate the Web.** Use the IE navigation features to jump from one site to another, go back to places you've been (via the Favorites and History features), and search for new places to visit.

➡ **Download files to your computer or print.** When you find what you want online, such as a graphic image or free software program, you can save it to your computer for future use. Do you need a hard copy of what you've found? Just use Internet Explorer's Print feature.

➡ **Protect yourself.** The Internet is a bit dangerous — a place where some people try to get to your private information and make nefarious use of it. IE provides privacy settings and special features to control the use of *cookies* (small files that folks insert on your hard drive that help them track your online activities). You also can use the Content Advisor to limit the online locations that your computer can visit.

Chapter 16

Get ready to . . .

Navigate the Web

1. Open IE by double-clicking the Internet Explorer icon on the Windows XP desktop. Depending on how you connect, a dialog box may appear asking you to log on to your dialup or other connection.

2. Enter a Web site address in the Address bar (enter a search engine such as Yahoo!, for example) and click Go, as shown in Figure 16-1.

3. On the resulting Web site, click a link or enter another address to proceed to another page.

 A link can be an icon or text. A text link is identifiable by colored text, usually blue or purple. After you click a link, it usually changes color to show that it's been followed.

4. Click the Back button to move back to the first page that you visited. Click the Forward button to go forward to the second page that you visited.

5. Click the down-pointing arrow to the right of the Back button to display a list of sites visited recently, as shown in Figure 16-2. Click a site in this list to go there.

 The Stop and Refresh buttons on the Standard toolbar are useful for navigating sites. Clicking the Stop button stops any page that is loading. So, if you made a mistake entering the address or if a page takes longer than you'd like to load, click the Stop button to halt the process. Clicking the Refresh button redisplays the current page. This is especially useful if a page updates information frequently, such as on a stock market site. You can also use Refresh if a page doesn't load correctly; it might just load correctly when refreshed.

Figure 16-1: Entering an address in the Address bar

Figure 16-2: Recently visited sites

Search the Web

1. Open IE and click the Search button on the Standard toolbar.

2. In the resulting Search pane, make sure that the Find a Web Page option is selected; enter a search term in the text box and then click Go.

3. In the resulting list of links or thumbnail pictures (depending on settings), click a link to go to that Web page. If you don't see the link that you need and more than one page of results is displayed, scroll down (if necessary) to click the link labeled Next to move to the next page.

4. If necessary, click the New button at the top of the Search pane to clear the search term; then enter a new search term.

5. Click the Customize button to set your search options.

6. In the resulting Customize Search Settings dialog box, as shown in Figure 16-3, select one the following options and then click OK to apply it:

   - **Use Search Assistant:** Select this option and then select the categories that you want to use to search. After you click OK, your new categories are displayed in the Search pane.

   - **Use One Search Service:** Select this option and then select a search service such as Google, Yahoo!, Lycos, or Excite from the list that appears. Click OK, and that search service becomes the default engine for the Search pane.

   - **Use Search Companion:** Select this option and refine your search by specifying items or locations.

   Figure 16-4 shows the results of selecting MSN as the search service, entering the question, What is the capital of Brazil?, and clicking Go.

Figure 16-3: The Customize Search Settings dialog box

 Knowing how search engines work can save you time. For example, if you search by entering **golden retriever**, you typically get sites that contain both words or either word. If you put a plus sign between these two keywords (golden+retriever), you get only sites that contain both words.

Figure 16-4: Search Companion results displayed

Find Content on a Web Page

1. With IE open and the Web page that you want to search displayed, choose Edit⇨Find (on This Page).

2. In the resulting dialog box, as shown in Figure 16-5, enter the word that you want to search for. Use the following options to narrow your results:

   - **Match Whole Word Only:** Select this option if you want to find only the whole word (for example, if you enter **cat** and want to find only *cat* and not *catatonic* or *catastrophe*).

   - **Match Case:** Select this option if you want to match the case (for example, if you enter **Catholic** and want to find only the always-capitalized religion and not the adjective *catholic*).

3. In the Direction area, select Up if you want to search the beginning of the page first; select Down if you want the end of the page to be searched first.

4. Click the Find Next button. The first instance of the word is highlighted on the page (see Figure 16-6). If you want to find another instance, click the Find Next button again.

5. When you're done searching, click the Cancel button in the Find dialog box.

 Many Web sites, such as www.amazon.com, have a Search feature that allows you to search not only the displayed Web page but all Web pages on the Web site. Look for a Search text box or link and make sure that it searches the site and not the entire Internet.

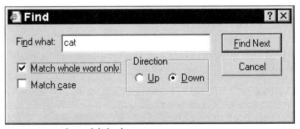

Figure 16-5: The Find dialog box

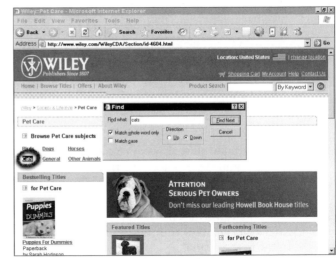

Figure 16-6: A found word highlighted on a Web page

Set Up a Home Page

1. Open IE and choose Tools⇨Internet Options.

2. In the resulting Internet Options dialog box, on the General tab, enter a Web site address to use as your home page, as shown in Figure 16-7, and then click OK. (My home page is shown in Figure 16-8 — pretty, isn't it?)

3. Alternatively, click one of the following preset option buttons, as shown in Figure 16-7:

   - **Use Current:** Sets whatever page is currently displayed in the browser window as your home page.

   - **Use Default:** This setting sends you to the MSN Web page.

   - **Use Blank:** If you're a minimalist, this setting is for you. No Web page displays — just a blank area.

4. Click the Home Page icon on the Internet Explorer toolbar (shaped like a little house) to go to your home page.

 What makes a good home page? Well, if you absolutely always check the news when you first log on, how about a news site such as CNN.com? Or, if you spend a lot of time online researching a topic, select a site with links to information about that topic (Genealogy.com, for example). Just want a fun jumping off point for the whole Internet? Online provider sites such as MSN.com or Yahoo.com often provide customizable home pages that let you include the topics of interest to you, such as horoscopes, news, local weather, shopping links, or sports.

Figure 16-7: Internet Options dialog box

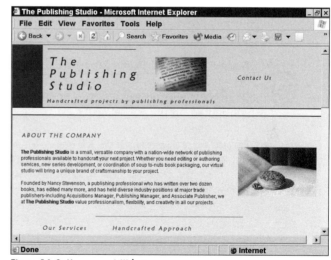

Figure 16-8: My company's Web site

Add a Web Site to Favorites

1. Open IE, enter the URL of a Web site that you want to add to your Favorites list, and then click Go.

2. Choose Favorites⇨Add to Favorites.

3. In the resulting Add Favorite dialog box, as shown in Figure 16-9, modify the name of the Favorite listing to be something easily recognizable. Click OK to add the site.

4. You can go to a favorite site in a couple of different ways:

   • Choose the Favorites menu and then click the name of the site from the list that displays.

   • Click the Favorites button on the Standard toolbar, and your favorites are displayed in the Favorite pane (see Figure 16-10). Click one to go there.

 Regularly clearing out your Favorites list is a good idea — after all, do you really need the sites that you used to plan last year's vacation? Choose Favorites⇨Organize Favorites. In the resulting dialog box, click a site to select it, and then delete it.

 One great way to organize favorite sites is to create folders within Favorites. In the Add Favorite dialog box, click the New Folder button. You can then choose that folder in the list before saving favorite sites that fit that category.

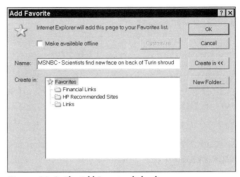

Figure 16-9: The Add Favorite dialog box

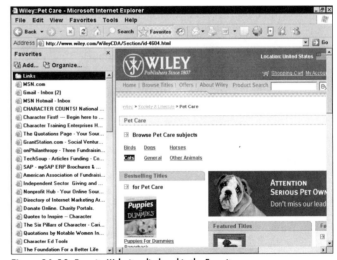

Figure 16-10: Favorite Web sites displayed in the Favorites pane

Organize Favorites

1. With Internet Explorer open, choose Favorites⇨Organize Favorites.

2. In the resulting Organize Favorites dialog box (see Figure 16-11), click the Create Folder, Rename, Move to Folder, or Delete button to organize your favorites.

3. With a favorite Web page highlighted, select the Make Available Offline check box (that appears in the text box below the buttons) to view the last displayed version of the Web page even after you log off of your Internet connection.

4. When you finish organizing your Favorites, click Close.

 These steps provide a handy way to manage several sites or folders, but you can also organize favorite sites one by one using the Favorites pane. Display the Favorites pane by clicking the Favorites button on the Standard toolbar. Right-click any favorite site listed in the pane and choose a command: Create New Folder, Delete, Rename, or Make Available Offline. You can also reorganize folders in the Favorites pane by dragging the icons up or down in the list.

 In the Add Favorite dialog box, if you right-click on a favorite, you can choose the Make Available Offline command. This allows you to access the page, though it won't be active or allow you to navigate the site. Essentially, it lets you look at the version of the page you last accessed as a kind of picture. This might be just enough if the favorite is an article, for example, that you want to be able to read offline.

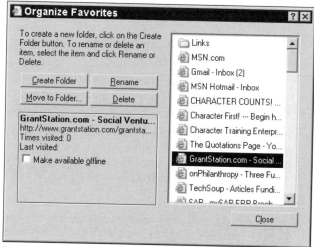

Figure 16-11: The Organize Favorites dialog box

View Your Browsing History

1. Choose View⇨Explorer Bar⇨History to display sites you've visited previously.

2. In the resulting History pane, click the arrow on the View button to show all viewing options. (The default view is By Date.)

3. With By Date view selected (as shown in Figure 16-12), click one of the folders in the list to display all sites in a particular time period, such as Last Week or 2 Weeks Ago. If you want to revisit a site in the list, click it, and you're there.

 To clear the IE History feature, choose Tools⇨Internet Options. On the General tab, click the Clear History button. To change how many days of searching the History feature saves, on the General tab, change the Days to Keep Pages in History setting by clicking the up or down spinner arrow. You can also delete a single site or folder from the History pane by right-clicking it and choosing Delete.

 You can quickly add a site you view in the History pane to your Favorites. Right-click on the site in the History pane and choose Add to Favorites. That's it!

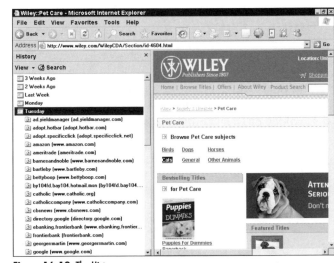

Figure 16-12: The History pane

Customize Internet Explorer

1. Open IE.

2. In the resulting home page, customize settings as follows:

- **Select text size.** Choose View⇨Text Size (see Figure 16-13) and select the size text you want displayed.

- **Personalize the Explorer bar.** Choose View⇨Explorer Bar and click an item from the list that you want to include in the Explorer Bar area on the left side of the IE screen, as shown in Figure 16-14.

 Displaying the History pane in the Explorer bar is useful, but here's a shortcut for visiting recently viewed sites: You can find Web pages that you've visited (up to nine of them) by clicking the arrow to the side of the Back button and choosing one from the list that's displayed.

- **Add toolbars.** Choose View⇨Toolbars. Try out all the toolbars in the list to see which ones you want to display. (Figure 16-14 shows all available toolbars displayed. Note that you can also include any third-party toolbars you might have added. For example, you can add the Google toolbar to IE by downloading it from www.google.com.)

 You can resize the various panes of Internet Explorer, such as the main Web page view pane and Explorer bar. Move your mouse over the vertical divider between panes until the cursor becomes a line with arrows on both sides; then click and drag the divider to enlarge or shrink a pane.

Figure 16-13: Changing text size

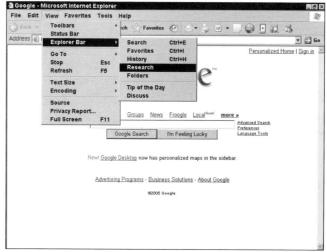

Figure 16-14: Explorer bar showing the Research pane

Download Files

1. Open a Web site with downloadable files. Some Web sites offer a Download Now button, and others provide a link to download a file.

2. Click the appropriate link to proceed.

3. In the resulting File Download dialog box, as shown in Figure 16-15, choose either of these options:

   - **Click Run to download to a temporary folder.** You can run an installation program for software, for example. However, beware: If you run a program directly from the Internet, you could introduce dangerous viruses to your system. Consider setting up an antivirus program to scan files before downloading them.

   - **Click Save to save the file to your hard drive.** In the Save As dialog box, select the folder on your computer or removable storage media (a CD-ROM, for example) where you want to save the file. If you're downloading software, you need to locate the downloaded file and click it to run the installation.

 Click Cancel in the File Download dialog box if you're worried that a particular file might be unsafe to download.

Change Privacy Settings

1. With IE open, choose Tools⇨Internet Options and click the Privacy tab, as shown in Figure 16-16.

2. Click the slider and drag it up or down to make different levels of security settings.

3. Read the choices and select a setting that suits you. Click OK to save it.

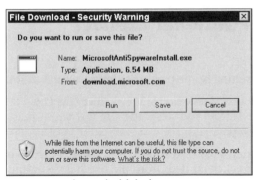

Figure 16-15: The Download dialog box

 The default Privacy setting — Medium — is probably a good bet for most people. To restore the default setting, click the Default button in the Internet Options dialog box Privacy sheet or use the slider to move back to Medium.

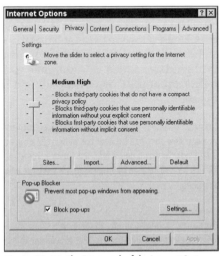

Figure 16-16: The Privacy tab of the Internet Options dialog box

Enable Content Advisor

1. With IE open, choose Tools⇨Internet Options.

2. In the resulting Internet Options dialog box, click the Content tab to display it.

3. Click the Enable button. (**Note:** If there is no Enable button but Disable and Settings buttons instead, Content Advisor is already enabled. Click the Settings button to see the options and make changes if you wish.)

4. On the Ratings tab of the Content Advisor dialog box (see Figure 16-17), click one of the four options: Language, Nudity, Sex, or Violence. Use the slider to set the site-screening level that's appropriate for you.

5. Repeat Step 4 for each of the categories.

6. Click the Approved Sites tab (see Figure 16-18) and enter the name of a specific site that you want to control access to. Then click either of the following options:

   • **Always:** Allows users to view the site, even if it's included in the Content Advisor screening level you've set.

   • **Never:** Means that nobody can visit the site even if it's acceptable to Content Advisor.

7. When you finish making your settings, click OK twice to save them.

 If you want to view sites that you don't want others to see, you can do that, too. On the General tab of the Content Advisor dialog box, make sure that the Supervisor Can Type a Password to Allow Viewers to View Restricted Content check box is selected. Then click Create Password. In the dialog box that appears, enter the password, confirm it, enter a hint, and click OK. Now if you're logged on as the system administrator, you can get to any restricted site by using this password.

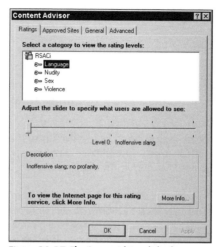

Figure 16-17: The Content Advisor dialog box

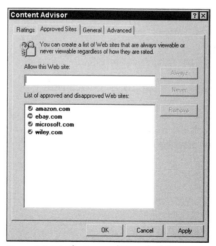

Figure 16-18: The Approved Sites tab of the Content Advisor

Print a Web Page

1. If a Web page includes a link or button to print or display a print version of a page, click that and follow the instructions.

2. If the page doesn't include a link for printing, simply press Ctrl+P.

3. In the resulting Print dialog box, decide how much of the document you want to print and click one of the options in the Page Range area, as shown in Figure 16-19.

 Choosing Current Page or entering page numbers in the Pages text box of the Print dialog box doesn't mean much when printing a Web page; the whole document might print anyway because Web pages aren't divided into pages the way word processor documents are.

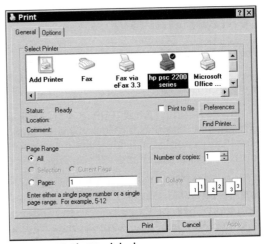

Figure 16-19: The Print dialog box

4. Click the up arrow in the Number of Copies text box to print multiple copies. If you want multiple copies collated, select the Collate check box.

5. Click the Options tab and change settings related to printing frames and links for the page.

6. When you've adjusted all settings, click Print.

 Another option for printing a page that doesn't offer a print version link is to right-click anywhere on the page and choose Print from the shortcut menu that appears.

Exchanging E-Mail with Outlook Express

Once upon a time, people spoke face to face or over the telephone, but that's all changed. Now the place to communicate with others is online.

E-mail is the *grand dame* of online communication. I bet that you've sent an e-mail or two in your time (unless you're a die-hard technophobe), but you might not be familiar with the ins and outs of using *Outlook Express,* which is the mini-version of the Outlook e-mail program from Microsoft that's built into Windows XP.

To pave the way to your e-mailing future, this chapter takes a look at the following tasks:

➠ **Receive, send, and forward messages.** Deal with the ins and outs of receiving and sending e-mail. Use the formatting tools that Outlook Express provides to make your messages look sharp.

➠ **Add information into the Address Book.** You can quickly and easily manage your contacts as well as organize the messages that you save in e-mail folders.

➠ **Set up the layout of all Outlook Express features.** Use the Folder bar and Layout features to create a very efficient workspace.

➠ **Manage your e-mail account.** Set up an e-mail account, and then create, modify, and add rules — these are like little instructions to Outlook Express for how to handle different situations, such as what to do when you get junk mail — by which your account should operate.

Chapter 17

Get ready to . . .

Open Outlook and Receive Messages

1. Choose Start➪Outlook Express or click the Outlook Express icon on your desktop.

2. In the Outlook Express window, press Ctrl+M to send and receive all messages.

3. Click the Inbox item in the Folders list to view messages. New messages display a small closed envelope icon; those with attachments display a paperclip icon as well (see Figure 17-1).

 To organize messages in the Inbox, click any of the headings at the top, such as From (to sort the messages alphabetically by sender), Received (to sort by the date messages were received), and so on.

 If you have Windows XP Service Pack 2 installed, you will be alerted about attachments that might be harmful when you try to open a message, such as an executable file or macro that might contain a virus. In addition, pictures in e-mails might be blocked from downloading to your computer; you can click a red X displayed in the e-mail labeled Click Here to Download Pictures to have them appear in the e-mail.

Create and Send E-Mail

1. Choose Start➪Outlook Express.

2. Click the Create Mail button on the Outlook toolbar to create a new blank e-mail form (as shown in Figure 17-2).

3. Type the e-mail address of the recipient in the To text box; to send a copy of the message to someone else, enter an e-mail address in the Cc field text box.

4. Click in the Subject text box and type a concise (yet descriptive) subject.

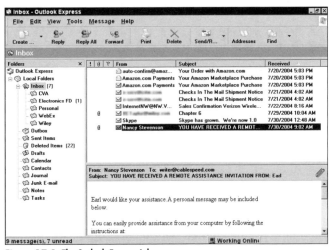

Figure 17-1: The Outlook Express Inbox

Figure 17-2: A new, blank e-mail form with addresses entered

5. Click in the message window and type your message (see Figure 17-3).

6. When you finish typing your message, spell-check it (unless you're the regional state spelling champ). Click the Spelling button in the e-mail form; if there's a possible misspelling, the word is highlighted, and the Spelling dialog box appears (see Figure 17-4). At this point, you have some choices:

- **Ignore:** Ignore this instance of the misspelling.

- **Ignore All:** Ignore all instances of the misspelling.

- **Change/Change All:** Click a suggested alternate spelling and then click the Change button to change that instance. Or, click the Change All button to change all instances of the word.

- **Add:** Add the current spelling of the word to the Spelling feature dictionary so it's never questioned again.

7. When you finish the spelling check, click the Send button. The message goes on its way!

 If the message is really urgent, you might also click the Priority button to add a bright red exclamation mark to the message header to alert the recipient. Click twice more to return the priority to low.

 When creating an e-mail, you can address it to a stored address by using the Address Book feature. Click the To button, and your Address Book appears. You can then select a contact. Outlook Express also allows you to just begin to type a stored contact in an address field (To or Cc), and it autofills likely options as you type. When it fills in the correct name, just press Enter to select it.

Figure 17-3: A message typed and ready to go

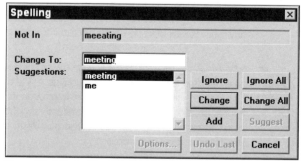

Figure 17-4: The Spelling dialog box

Send an Attachment

1. Create a new e-mail message, address it, and enter a subject.

2. Click the Attach button in the e-mail form toolbar.

3. In the Insert Attachment dialog box that appears (see Figure 17-5), locate the document that you want by using the Look In drop-down list and the File Name text box. Select the document and then click Attach.

4. With the name of the attached file now in the Attach text box (see Figure 17-6), type a message (or not — after all, a picture *is* worth a thousand words).

5. Click Send.

 If you want to send somebody your own contact information, create a business card in your Address Book and attach it to an e-mail. This is saved in *vCard* format, which the recipient can then import into his or her Address Book. First create yourself as a contact. Then, in the Address Book window, choose File⇨Export⇨Business Card and save it. Now you can attach the vCard to any e-mail, any time.

 Some e-mail programs limit the size of a message and its attachment, so a larger attachment just might not get through. To change the size of messages that you can send, choose Tools⇨Accounts; on the Mail tab, click Properties. On the Advanced tab, select Break Apart Messages Larger Than *x* and enter the maximum file size that your e-mail server can accommodate.

Figure 17-5: The Insert Attachment dialog box

Figure 17-6: The Attach field showing an attached file

Read a Message

1. Double-click an e-mail message in your Inbox. Unread messages display an unopened envelope icon to the left of the message subject.

2. Use the scrollbars in the message window to scroll down through the message and read it (see Figure 17-7).

3. An attachment to a message is shown as a paper clip symbol when the message is closed in your Inbox (see Figure 17-1); attachments are listed in the Attach box in the open message (see Figure 17-6). To open an attachment, double-click it.

4. In the Open Attachment Warning dialog box (see Figure 17-8), select the Open It radio button and then click OK. The attachment opens in whatever program is associated with it (such as the Windows Fax and Picture Viewer for a graphics file) or the program it was created in (such as Word for Windows XP).

 If you'd rather save an attachment to a storage disk or your hard drive, when the Open Attachment Warning dialog box opens, select the Save It To Disk. In the Save As dialog box that appears, choose a location and provide a name for the file, and then click Save.

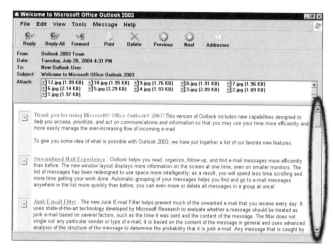

Figure 17-7: Use the scrollbar to see more of a long e-mail message

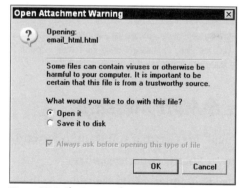

Figure 17-8: The Open Attachment Warning dialog box

Reply to a Message

1. With the message you want to reply to open, select one of the following reply options:

   • **Reply:** Send the reply to only the author.

   • **Reply All:** Send a reply to the author as well as everyone who received the original message.

2. In the resulting e-mail form (see Figure 17-9), enter a new recipient(s) in the To and/or Cc text boxes and type your message in the message window area.

3. Click the Send button to send the reply.

 If you don't want to include the original message in your reply, choose Tools⇨Options and click the Send tab. Clear the Include Message in Reply check box to deselect it, and then click OK.

 To be sure the person you reply to can view the message in his or her browser, you can arrange to reply in the format in which the message was sent to you. Choose Tools⇨Options and click the Send tab. Click the Reply to Messages Using the Format in Which They Were Sent check box to select it, and then click OK.

Forward an E-Mail Message

1. Open the e-mail message that you want to forward.

2. Click the Forward button on the toolbar.

3. In the message that appears with *Fw* added to the beginning of the subject line, enter a new recipient(s) in the To and Cc text boxes and then enter any message that you want to include in the message window area, as shown in the example in Figure 17-10.

4. Click Send to forward the message.

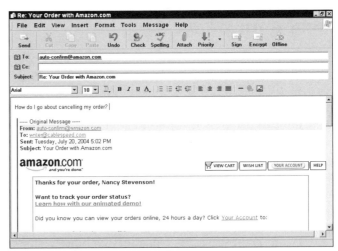

Figure 17-9: Add your message as a reply

Figure 17-10: A message ready to be forwarded

Create and Add a Signature

1. Choose Tools⇨Options to open the Options dialog box. Click the Signatures tab (see Figure 17-11).

2. Click the New button to create a new signature and then enter the Signatures text.

3. Select the Add Signatures to All Outgoing Messages check box and make sure that the signature is selected as the default. (**Note:** Select the Don't Add Signatures to Replies and Forwards check box to insert a signature manually. If you want to add the signature only occasionally, I suggest you go this route.)

4. Click OK to save the signature. To manually add a signature to an open e-mail message click in the message to place your cursor where you want the signature to appear, choose Insert⇨Signature and select a signature from the list that appears to insert it (see Figure 17-12).

 Here's how to to assign a different signature to each account if you have different e-mail accounts: When you're on the Signatures tab of the Options dialog box, select a signature from the Signatures list box, click the Advanced button, and then select an account to associate it with.

Figure 17-11: The Options dialog box, Signatures tab

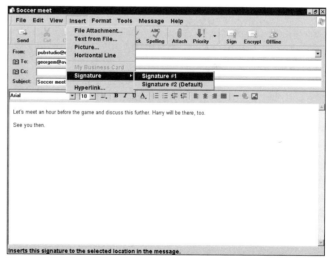

Figure 17-12: Manually inserting a signature in an e-mail

Format an E-Mail Message

1. Create a new e-mail message or open a message and click Reply or Forward.

2. Select (highlight) the text that you want to format (see Figure 17-13).

3. Use any of the following options to make changes to the font. (See the toolbar containing these tools in Figure 17-13, and a message with various formats applied in Figure 17-14.)

   • **Font drop-down list:** Select an option from this list to apply it to the text.

   • **Font Size drop-down list:** Change the font size here.

   • **Paragraph Style button:** Apply a preset style, such as Heading 1 or Address.

   • **Bold, Italic, or Underline buttons:** Apply styles to selected text.

   • **Font Color button:** Display a color palette and click a color to apply it to selected text.

   • **Formatting Numbers or Formatting Bullets buttons:** Apply numbering order to lists or precede each item with a round bullet.

   • **Align Left, Center, Align Right, or Justify buttons:** Adjust the alignment of the text.

   • **Increase Indentation or Decrease Indentation button:** Indent a paragraph to the right or move it to the left.

   • **Insert Horizontal Line button:** Add a line to your message.

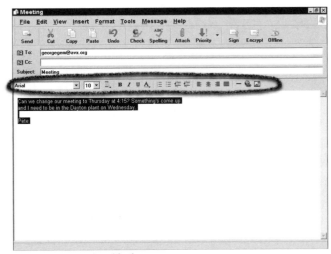

Figure 17-13: Text selected for formatting

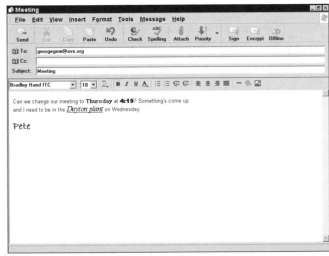

Figure 17-14: A variety of formats applied to an e-mail message

Add Stationery

1. Click the arrow on the Create Mail button in the Outlook Express main window and select a stationery option listed in the menu that appears, or choose the Select Stationery command to get more choices.

2. In the Select Stationery dialog box that appears (see Figure 17-15), select a stationery from the list.

3. Click OK to apply the stationery to the new message.

4. With a new, reply, or forwarded message open, you can also apply stationery by choosing Format⇨Apply Stationery and then click a stationery to apply (see Figure 17-16).

You can edit stationery, for example to add or delete a graphic element. In the Select Stationery dialog box, click on the stationery you want to change and click the Edit button. The stationery opens in a Word document that offers various tools you can use to insert and format text or pictures.

If you apply stationery and decide that you don't want to use it anymore, just click the arrow on the Create button and select No Stationery from the drop-down list.

Figure 17-15: The Select Stationery dialog box

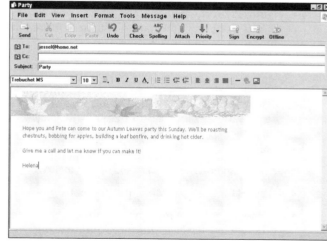

Figure 17-16: Stationery applied to an e-mail message

Add Contacts to the Address Book

1. In the Outlook Express main window, click the Addresses button to open the Address Book window.

2. To create a new contact in the resulting Address Book window, as shown in Figure 17-17, click the New button and then choose New Contact from the menu that appears. (**Note:** New Group can be used to create a group of people from existing contacts, such as your car pool members.)

3. In the resulting Properties dialog box, as shown in Figure 17-18, you select from the following options tabs to enter contact information:

   • **Name:** Enter the person's name and e-mail address. (This is the only information you are required to enter to create a contact.)

   • **Home:** Enter the person's home address, phone, fax, cellphone, and Web site.

   • **Business:** Enter information about the company that the person works for, his or her job title, pager number, and even a map to help you find his or her office.

   • **Personal:** Enter the person's family members' names, as well as gender, birthday, and anniversary.

   • **Other:** Use this space for miscellaneous notes.

   • **NetMeeting:** Insert information about the person's conferencing server if you meet online using Microsoft's NetMeeting.

   • **Digital IDs:** Ensure secure communications. *Digital IDs* are certificates that you can use to verify the identity of the person with whom you're communicating.

4. Click OK to save your new contact information and close the Address Book.

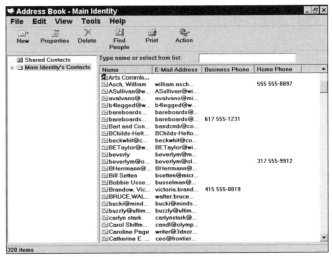

Figure 17-17: The Address Book window

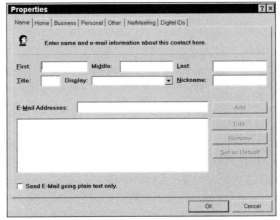

Figure 17-18: The Name tab of the Properties dialog box

Customize the Outlook Express Window Layout

1. Choose View⇨Layout to open the Window Layout Properties dialog box.

2. Mark various check boxes in the Basic section (top of Figure 17-19) to select items to display in separate panes (as shown in Figure 17-20), including:

   - **Contacts:** A list of all the contacts in your Address Book. Click any contact to address a new or forwarded message.

   - **Folder Bar:** A bar near the top of the screen that includes a drop-down list of folders.

   - **Folder List:** A pane containing a list of all folders.

   - **Outlook Bar:** A vertical bar that includes icons for accessing your Inbox, Outbox, Sent Items, Deleted Items, and Drafts.

   - **Status Bar:** The bar across the bottom of the screen that lists the number of messages in all your folders and the number of unread messages.

   - **Toolbar:** The bar containing tools you use to create and work with messages, such as Create, Reply, Forward, and Print.

   - **Views Bar:** A bar under the toolbar containing a drop-down menu with three commands: Hide Read Messages, Hide Read or Ignored Messages, and Show All Messages.

3. Click various options in the Preview Pane section (bottom of Figure 17-19) to preview a message selected in the Inbox, Outbox, Drafts, Sent Items, or Deleted Items folders.

4. Click OK to apply and save all your layout settings.

Figure 17-19: The Window Layout Properties dialog box

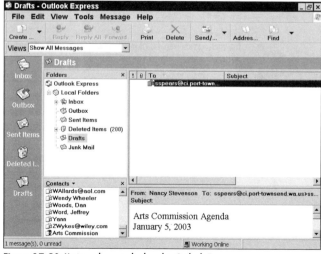

Figure 17-20: Various elements displayed in Outlook Express

Create Message Folders

1. Choose File⇨New⇨Folder.

2. In the resulting Create Folder dialog box (see Figure 17-21), click to select the parent folder that you want the new folder to be created under and then enter a new folder name.

3. Click OK.

Typically, you select the Local Folders item in Step 5 so that the new folder is at the same level as the Inbox, Outbox, and so on. Alternatively, you could select the Inbox item to place the new folder within the Inbox folder.

Don't rely on messages stored in Outlook folders as your main storage space. Should you have serious system problems, you have a better chance restoring files stored in Windows XP folders than those stored in Outlook Express.

You can rename a folder at any time after you create it. Just right-click on it and choose Rename, and then enter a new name in the Rename Folder dialog box that appears and click OK.

Figure 17-21: The Create Folder dialog box

Organize Messages in Folders

1. In the Folders list, click a plus sign to the left of any folder to display its contents (see Figure 17-22).

2. To place a message in a folder, you can do one of these actions:

   - **Click and drag.** With a folder (such as the Inbox) displayed, click a message and drag it into a folder in the Folders list.

   - **Move an open message.** With an e-mail message open, choose File⇨Move to Folder or Copy to Folder. In the Move dialog box that appears (see Figure 17-23), select the appropriate folder and click OK.

   - **Move a closed message.** Right-click a message in a displayed folder and choose Move to Folder or Copy to Folder. In the dialog box that appears, select the appropriate folder and click OK.

3. To delete a message, display the folder it's saved in, select the message and then either click the Delete button or press Delete on the keyboard.

 If you try to delete a message from your Deleted Items folder, a message appears asking whether you really want to delete this message permanently. That's because when you delete a message from another folder, it's really not deleted — it's simply placed in the Deleted Items folder. To send it into oblivion, you have to delete it from the Deleted Items folder, confirming your deletion so that Outlook Express is really convinced that you mean what you say.

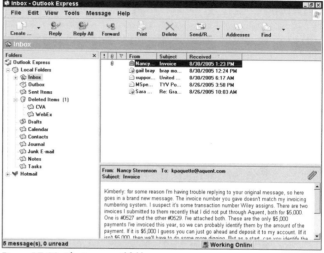

Figure 17-22: Files in an e-mail folder

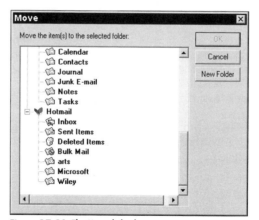

Figure 17-23: The Move dialog box

Manage an E-Mail Account

1. In the Outlook Express main window, choose Tools⇨ Accounts.

2. In the resulting Internet Accounts dialog box, as shown in Figure 17-24, set up a new account by clicking one of the following tabs:

   • **Mail:** For e-mail accounts

   • **News:** For newsgroups

   • **Directory Service:** For online search services used by the Address Book to search for people

   • **All:** all three existing account types are listed on this single tab, and you can also create any account type with this tab displayed.

3. Click the Add button and choose the appropriate service.

4. In the resulting Internet Connection Wizard (see Figure 17-25), follow the set-up steps.

   Following the Internet Connection Wizard often requires that you provide certain information about your Internet service provider (ISP), such as its mail server or connection method. Keep this information handy!

5. To remove an account, click the Remove button on any of the tabs. A confirming message appears. To delete the account, click Yes.

6. Select an account and click the Set As Default button to make it the account that Windows XP connects you to whenever you go online. In the case of the mail server, the default is the one used to send any messages.

7. When you finish setting up accounts, click the Close button to close the Internet Accounts dialog box.

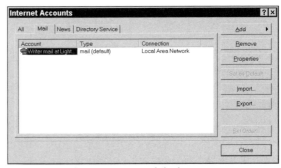

Figure 17-24: The Internet Accounts dialog box

If you've installed Windows XP Service Pack 2, it has a feature that prevents others from validating your e-mail address without your knowledge. If somebody tries to download something when you open your e-mail (often a file that allows the sender to get an automatic reply from active e-mail accounts), you are alerted and offered the option of not allowing the download.

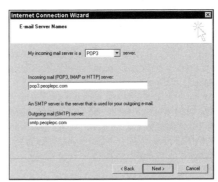

Figure 17-25: The Internet Connection Wizard

Create Mail Rules

1. Choose Tools⇨Message Rules⇨Mail.

2. In the resulting New Mail Rule dialog box (see Figure 17-26), mark check boxes to set Conditions for your rule (for example, all messages where the subject line contains specific words, such as *Sale* or *Free*).

3. Mark check boxes to select an Action for the rule. In the example in Step 2, for instance, you might select the Move It To The Specified Folder option.

4. In the Rule Description area, click the link (the colored text). Fill in the specific information for the rule in the dialog box that appears. (See Figure 17-27 for an example where you enter the word **sale** to move e-mail with that word in the subject to another folder.)

5. Fill in the Name of the Rule text box with a name that you can recognize, and then click OK.

 After you create a rule, open the Message Rules dialog box by choosing Tools⇨Message Rules⇨Mail and then in the Message dialog box click on the rule you want to change. Click the Modify button to make changes to the rule, or click the Remove button to delete it.

 Here are some rules that people find handy to create: Place messages marked as priority in a Priority folder or put messages with attachments in an Attachments folder. When you're on vacation, choose to have all messages forwarded to somebody else, such as an assistant; or, if a message is from a certain person, mark it with a color. ***Note:*** If you use the autoforward feature, you have to leave your computer on and also leave Outlook Express open while you're away.

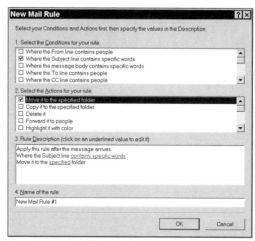

Figure 17-26: Specify rule details

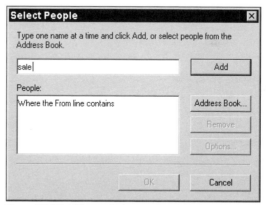

Figure 17-27: Add a specific description

Part V
Networking

The 5th Wave   By Rich Tennant

"Since we got it, he hasn't moved from that spot for eleven straight days. Oddly enough they call this 'getting up and running' on the internet."

Setting Up a Network

Setting up a network among two or more computers can make your life much easier because, after you set up a network, you can use this connection to share files, folders, and access to the Internet with other users. (See Chapter 19 for more about how to do this.)

The most common way to connect a network is to use a wired Ethernet connection, involving cables and equipment, referred to as a *hub* or *switch*. To determine whether your computer is Ethernet-ready, check the back of your PC: You should see what looks like a very large phone connector jack. This is the Ethernet connector.

After you connect the necessary cables and equipment, many newer computers already have network drivers installed, so Windows XP is capable of recognizing the connection. With simple-to-use wizards, little input on your part is often required to set up a network.

You can also set up a connection through a wireless access point (which you set up according to the instructions that come with it) and an adapter that you either install in your CPU in the form of a PCI adapter or plug into your PC using a USB (Universal Serial Bus) port or PC Card adapter.

To set up a network, you explore the following tasks:

⇒ Installing a network adapter and configuring a network by using the Network Setup Wizard

⇒ Setting up a wireless access point and configuring a wireless network by using the Wireless Network Setup Wizard

⇒ Making various settings to a network connection, including verifying the connection; changing a networked computer's name so the one you gave it when you bought it (Hot Mama, Road Warrior, or whatever) isn't the one that shows on the network; and creating and viewing workgroups on a network

Chapter 18

Get ready to . . .

Install a PCI Network Adapter

1. After purchasing the PCI adapter, turn off your desktop computer and disconnect all power and other cables from it.

2. Open the PC chassis (see Figure 18-1). Check your user's manual for this procedure, which usually involves removing a few screws and popping the cover off your tower.

3. Touch a metal object to get rid of any static discharge before you reach inside the computer.

4. Locate the slots for the PCI adapter. Again, check your manual for the exact location in your system.

5. Remove the adapter from its packaging. Handling it by its edges, line it up with the slot and insert it firmly but gently.

6. Make sure you don't disconnect any wires or leave loose screws inside the PC chassis; then replace the computer cover and reinsert the screws.

 It's a good idea to leave parts you are going to insert in your computer in their packaging until you need them. If they sit around on your desktop or elsewhere they could pick up static discharge which could be harmful to your computer.

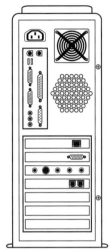

Figure 18-1: Opening your CPU case

 You can buy PCI network adapters in many large office supply or computer stores, or look for discount prices at online providers such as Amazon.com/electronics.

7. Plug in the computer and turn it on. Your computer should sense the new adapter when it starts up and display the Found New Hardware pop-up above your taskbar.

8. Click the pop-up. In the resulting Found New Hardware Wizard (see Figure 18-2), follow the steps. If Windows XP cannot find a driver for the adapter, you might have to provide it.

9. When you complete the wizard, a new Found New Hardware pop-up appears stating that your hardware driver is installed and ready to use.

 If your computer doesn't automatically sense the new adapter, go to the Printers and Other Hardware section of Control Panel and click the Add Hardware link in the See Also pane. This displays the Add New Hardware Wizard, which guides you through the setup process.

 If Windows XP cannot find the driver, you can usually download it from your hardware manufacturer's Web site for free. Once you do, use the Browse button, locate the location where you downloaded the driver, and proceed with the wizard.

Figure 18-2: The Found New Hardware Wizard

Verify a Local Area Connection

1. Choose Start➪Control Panel➪Network And Internet Connections.

2. In the resulting Network and Internet Connections window, as shown in Figure 18-3, click the Network Connections link.

3. In the resulting Network Connections window, as shown in Figure 18-4, locate the Local Area Connection icon in the Name column; this indicates that your network adapter is properly installed and configured.

4. Click the Close button to close the Network Connections window.

 To see the status of a connection, double-click the icon in the Network Connections window. The Connection Status dialog box appears, telling you whether the connection is active and at what speed it's operating. On the Support tab of this dialog box, you can click the Repair button for help if the connection isn't operating properly.

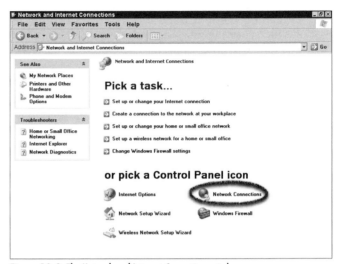

Figure 18-3: The Network and Internet Connections window

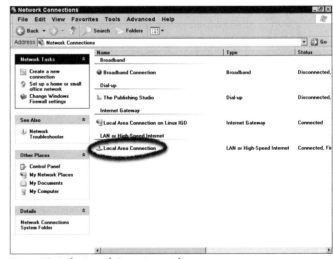

Figure 18-4: The Network Connections window

Connect a Wired Ethernet Network

1. Obtain a Cat 5 or Cat 5e Ethernet cable for every computer you will connect to the network (see Figure 18-5).

2. Purchase a hub or switch with enough ports for each computer you want to connect (see Figure 18-6).

3. Turn off all computers as well as the switch/hub and plug one end of the Ethernet cable into the switch or hub and the other end into the network adapter you installed in your PC. See the first task in this chapter for help with this.

4. Repeat Step 3 for each computer you want to include in the network.

5. Turn on the switch or hub and then turn on the computers. Use the following task to run the Network Setup Wizard and set up the network.

 Switches make for a speedier network although they cost a little more than a hub. However, in most cases, it's better to invest a few dollars more for the extra performance of a switch. If you want to get very sophisticated, for example on a company network, you could use a router, which helps you track various people on the network and the places they are going on the network.

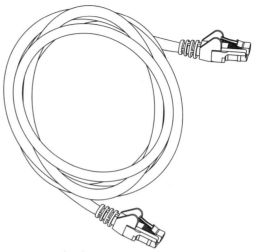

Figure 18-5: The Ethernet connector

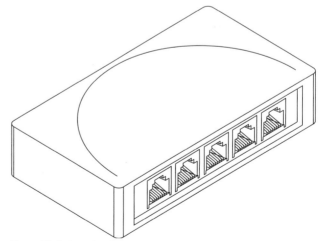

Figure 18-6: A switch with ports

Configure a Network by Using the Network Setup Wizard

1. Turn on each PC that you have attached to the network.

2. On the PC that will share its Internet connection, log on to the Internet.

3. On the Internet-connection PC, choose Start⇨ All Programs⇨Accessories⇨Communications⇨ Network Setup Wizard.

4. In the resulting Network Setup Wizard window, click Next. Then, you can click on the checklist for creating a network link to review the checklist for the steps involved in setting up a network. After reviewing the list click Next again.

5. In the resulting Select A Connection Method window (see Figure 18-7), choose the option that matches how you connect to the Internet and then click Next. Depending on your choice, you might see a window where you select your specific Internet connection; then click Next.

 The Checklist for Creating a Network mentioned in Step 4 provides step-by-step information about all aspects of creating a network, including buying guides for the right network hardware to purchase to get your network going.

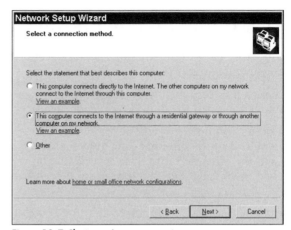

Figure 18-7: Sharing an Internet connection

 To confirm an Ethernet network connection use the Control Panel to open the Device Manager. Locate the network adapter, and double-click on it. Display the General tab to see if the device is enabled.

6. In the resulting window, enter a name for your computer and then click Next. The following window asks for your workgroup name. The default workgroup for your computer is already entered there, and you should click Next to accept it.

7. In the resulting window (see Figure 18-8), choose the option for file and printer sharing that you prefer and then click Next. A confirming dialog box lists your settings. Click Next to set up the connection.

8. The resulting window offers for you to create a setup CD for computers not using Windows XP. Assuming that all computers on your network are running Windows XP, choose the Just Finish the Wizard option and then click Next.

9. In the resulting final wizard screen, click Finish. A dialog box appears stating that you must restart the computer to complete the connection. Click Yes.

When you are offered the option of file and printer sharing by the wizard, it most often makes sense to allow sharing to occur. In most cases, that's a big part of why you create a network in the first place. However, if you are networked with other computers — say, to share an Internet connection — but you don't want others on the network to access your files for privacy reasons, choose to not share at that point in the wizard.

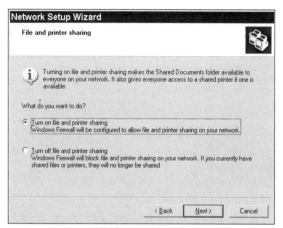

Figure 18-8: Choosing file sharing options

If you have computers on your network that are not using Windows XP, creating a setup CD in Step 8 above allows you to make settings in other operating system versions that correspond to the settings you have just set up.

Configure a Wireless Network with the Wireless Network Setup Wizard

1. Choose Start⇨All Programs⇨Accessories⇨ Communications⇨Wireless Network Setup Wizard.

2. In the resulting Wireless Network Setup Wizard, click Next.

3. In the Create a Name for Your Wireless Network window that appears (see Figure 18-9), type a name and verify that Automatically Assign A Network Key is selected. Click Next.

4. In the resulting How Do You Want to Setup Up Your Network? dialog box, as shown in Figure 18-10, choose one of two options:

   - **If you have a Flash drive connected via a USB port:** Connect the drive and choose Use a USB Flash Drive. Click Next and follow the directions which involve disconnecting the flash drive and plugging it into a wireless access point. You can then use the drive to configure each computer on the network as directed.

   - **If you prefer to set up each computer, one by one:** Choose the manual option by running the Wireless Network Setup Wizard on each and then clicking Next.

5. On the final wizard screen that appears, click Finish.

 When you purchase a wireless access point, it includes instructions for setting it up. This typically involves plugging it into a power source, plugging in Ethernet cables to your main computer and possibly a DSL (digital subscriber line) or other high-speed modem, and turning it on.

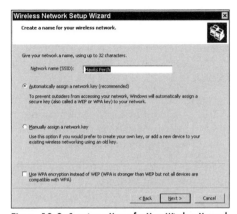

Figure 18-9: Creating a Name for Your Wireless Network

Figure 18-10: Choosing how to set up your network

Change a Computer's Network Name

1. Choose Start➪Control Panel➪Performance and Maintenance and then click the System link, as shown in Figure 18-11.

2. In the resulting System dialog box, click the Computer Name tab.

3. Click Change. In the resulting Computer Name Changes dialog box, as shown in Figure 18-12, type a name in the Computer Name text box and then click OK twice.

4. The dialog boxes close, and the new name is saved.

 Two computers on the same network cannot have the same name.

 Making the computer name descriptive is useful: Simple names such as John's Computer and Basement PC help everybody on the network know which is which.

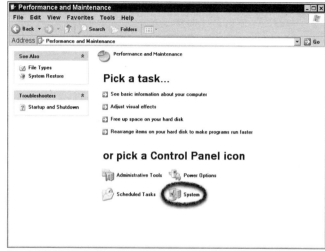

Figure 18-11: The Performance and Maintenance window of the Control Panel

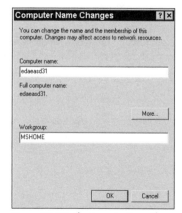

Figure 18-12: The Computer Name Changes dialog box

Join a Workgroup

1. Choose Start⇨Control Panel⇨Performance and Maintenance. Click the System link.

2. In the resulting System dialog box, click the Computer Name tab (see Figure 18-13).

3. Click the Change button to open the Computer Name Changes dialog box (see Figure 18-14). Type the name for your workgroup *with no spaces between letters*.

4. Click OK to close the dialog box, and then click OK again to close the System dialog box. If prompted, restart Windows XP.

 A *workgroup* is essentially a set of computers on a network. On a large network, breaking computers down into these groups so they can easily work with each other makes sense. In a smaller home network, you will probably just create one workgroup to allow all your computers to easily access each other.

 A workgroup name is restricted to 15 characters maximum. Also, the name can't contain the characters : ; " < > * + = \ | ? and ,.

Figure 18-13: The System dialog box, Computer Name tab

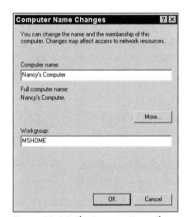

Figure 18-14: The Computer Name Changes dialog box

View Workgroup Computers

1. Choose Start⇨My Network Places.

2. In the resulting My Network Places window, as shown in Figure 18-15, click the View Workgroup Computers link from the Network Tasks pane.

3. In the resulting window, titled with the name of your network, you can view a list of all workgroup computers that are connected to the network, as shown in Figure 18-16. Only connected computers are listed here.

4. Click the Close button to close the window.

 When you view a workgroup, you can double-click one to see a listing of all the devices, scheduled tasks, and shared files and folders available to the group.

 If a computer in the workgroup is not connected, the Computer column in the My Network Places window will read "Unknown." When you next connect, the name of the computer will appear in this column.

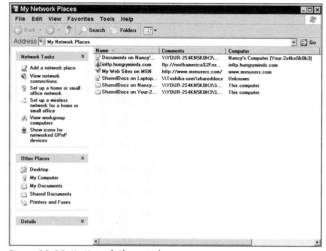

Figure 18-15: My Network Places window

Figure 18-16: The Workgroup Computers window showing the two computers on my home network

Connecting Across a Network

*A*fter you set up a network among your computers (see Chapter 18 for details about how to do this), you still have a few more things to set up so you work over your network connection — make settings to share files and printer, for example.

To work with your network efficiently and effectively, I show you how to perform the following tasks:

➡ After you verify that you are connected, you can *map* — that is allow your computer to make the connection between — a folder on one computer to another computer's disk drive. This allows other computers on the network to access the folder just as if it were a drive on their computer.

➡ In some cases, you have to turn off Windows Firewall to share, but most network router software provides its own firewall to keep your network secure.

➡ You can make settings to share a connection to a peripheral device, such as a printer or scanner. You can also use the Shared Documents folder to allow others access to specific files and folders.

Note that sharing your Internet connection happens automatically when you plug your high-speed modem into your network router and then run the Network Setup Wizard, making choices about how computers should connect to the Internet. See Chapter 18 for more about setting up a network.

Chapter 19

Get ready to . . .

Verify Network Connection Status

1. Choose Start⇨My Network Places. In the resulting My Network Places window (see Figure 19-1), click View Network Connections from the Network Tasks pane on the left.

2. In the resulting Network Connections window, double-click your network (probably labeled Local Area Connection).

3. On the General tab (see Figure 19-2) of the resulting Status dialog box, check that the status reads `Connected`. If the network is active and connected, you should see a number of packets listed as sent and received in the Activity section of the dialog box.

4. Click Close to close the dialog box.

 If you're not connected to your network, right-click the connection in the Network Connections window and choose the appropriate command. For example, a broadband connection might offer the command Connect while a wireless connection would offer Enable.

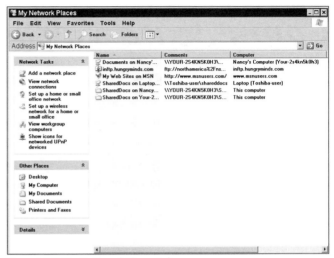

Figure 19-1: The My Network Places window

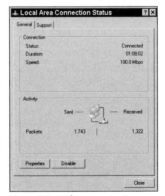

Figure 19-2: The connection Status dialog box

Map a Network Folder to a Drive

1. Choose Start⇨My Network Places. (***Note:*** You can actually open any folder in Windows Explorer to perform this task.)

2. Choose Tools⇨Map Network Drive.

3. In the resulting Map Network Drive dialog box, as shown in Figure 19-3, open the Drive drop-down list and choose a drive letter that corresponds to the drive you want to map to.

4. Click Browse. In the Browse for Folder dialog box (see Figure 19-4), locate the shared folder on the network that you want to map to a drive and then click OK.

5. Check that the Reconnect at Login check box is selected and then click Finish.

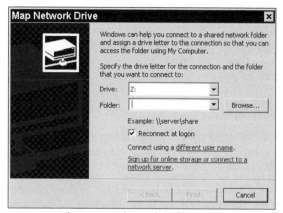

Figure 19-3: The Map Network Drive dialog box

To undo mapping of a folder, locate the folder in Windows Explorer and choose Tools⇨Disconnect Network Drive. In the dialog box that appears, simply click the icon of the drive you want to undo and then click OK.

You can't map to a network drive unless it has been set up to be shared on the other computer. To do so locate the drive in the My Computer window, right-click and choose Sharing and Security and make settings to share the drive in the resulting dialog box.

Figure 19-4: The Browse for Folder dialog box

Disable Windows Firewall

1. Choose Start➪Control Panel➪Network and Internet Connections.

2. In the resulting Network and Internet Connections window, as shown in Figure 19-5, click the Windows Firewall link.

3. On the General tab in the resulting Windows Firewall dialog box, as shown in Figure 19-6, select the Off radio button.

4. Click OK to save the setting. Be sure to now enable WEP or WPA protection in your router setup following your manufacturer's instructions.

 WEP stands for Wired Equivalency Privacy, and WPA stands for Wi-Fi Protected Access. Both are security protocols used to protect you from having other people tap into your wireless communications.

 In some cases, leaving the firewall on and selecting the File and Printer Sharing item on the Exceptions tab of the Windows Firewall dialog box is sufficient to allow sharing. If you can go that route, you should so that your computer can take advantage of Windows Firewall protection.

Figure 19-5: The Network and Internet Connections window

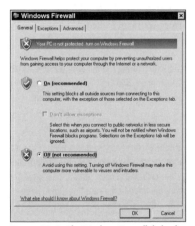

Figure 19-6: The Windows Firewall dialog box

Share Folders

1. Use Windows Explorer to locate the folder you want to share.

2. In the resulting window, right-click the folder (see Figure 19-7) and choose Sharing and Security.

3. In the Properties dialog box that appears, as shown in Figure 19-8, select the Share This Folder on the Network check box.

4. You can enter a share name for the folder. Do this if the folder name is long, but note that a networked computer that has a pre-Windows XP version of the Windows operating system might not recognize a file name longer than 12 characters.

5. If you want to allow others to make changes to files in this folder, select Allow Network Users to Change My Files.

6. Click OK to save settings and share the folder.

 If a folder or one of its parent folders is specified as private, you can't select the sharing option in the Properties dialog box. You can make folders in the Documents and Settings folder private or not private by using a setting in their respective Properties dialog box.

Figure 19-7: Setting up folder sharing

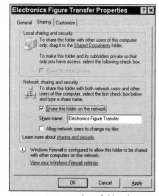

Figure 19-8: Finishing folder sharing setup

Remove Folder Sharing

1. Use Windows Explorer to locate the folder you want to unshare.

2. In the resulting window, right-click the folder and choose Sharing and Security.

3. In the Properties dialog box that appears, as shown in Figure 19-9, clear the Share This Folder on the Network check box to deselect it.

4. Click OK to save the setting.

 If you share any Windows XP folders or folders that contain program files, such as Microsoft Word, I recommend disabling sharing. You should also avoid sharing the root folder of your hard drive. Nobody on your network should need to get to these, and sharing them poses a security threat to your system.

 Note that you have to be at the computer whose folder you want to make unavailable on the network and logged in with admin rights to unshare a folder.

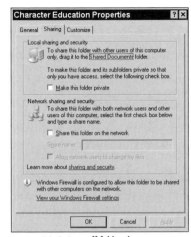

Figure 19-9: Turn off folder sharing

Share a Printer

1. Choose Start⇨Control Panel⇨Printers and Other Hardware⇨View Installed Printers or Fax Printers.

2. In the resulting Printers and Faxes window, click a printer in the list to select it and then choose File⇨Sharing.

3. In the resulting Properties dialog box, as shown in Figure 19-10, select the Share This Printer check box.

4. Click OK.

5. On each networked computer, go to the Printers and Faxes window and run the Add a Printer wizard. On the second wizard screen, as shown in Figure 19-11, select A Network Printer. When you click Next, Windows XP shows you a list of printers available on the network. Select the one you want to connect to and then proceed with the wizard.

 You can optionally change the printer name in the Properties dialog box. Providing a name that network users can most easily identify, such as Color Printer or Printer in Office, might work best.

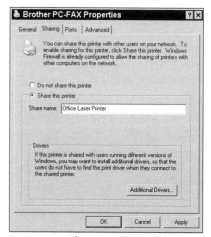

Figure 19-10: The printer Properties dialog box

Figure 19-11: The Add a Printer Wizard

Remove Printer Sharing

1. On the computer in the network that is locally connected to the printer, choose Start⇨Control Panel⇨Printers and Other Hardware⇨View Installed Printers or Fax Printers.

2. In the resulting Printers and Faxes window, click a printer in the list to select it and then choose File⇨ Sharing.

3. In the resulting Properties dialog box, as shown in Figure 19-12, select the Do Not Share This Printer check box to disable sharing it.

4. Click OK.

 Note that you have to be logged on with administrator rights to the computer that has the printer physically attached to it in order to remove a printer.

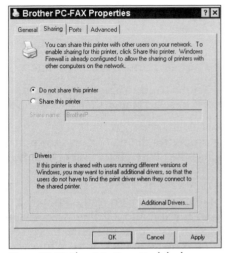

Figure 19-12: The printer Properties dialog box

Part VI
Security and Troubleshooting

Making Windows XP Secure

When you work with Windows XP and the software that it supports, you end up with lots of folders full of precious documents and data. Microsoft provides security features in Windows XP that help you keep all that information private, whether at work or home, and keeps you in trusted territory when you're online. You can do the following to keep your computer safe:

- ➡ **Use password protection.** Keep people from accessing your computer when you're not around. A Windows XP password stops people from logging on to Windows XP, and a screen saver password ensures that nobody can stop the screen saver from running without entering a password.

- ➡ **Share information.** Share folders with others on a network or keep others out of folders. You can also use the shared folders feature to share folders with multiple users of a standalone computer.

- ➡ **Protect individual files.** Make files *read-only* — that is, allow people to read what's in them but not make and save changes — or hide files from others entirely.

- ➡ **Set up Internet Explorer zones.** Designate trusted Web sites (which you have reason to believe are perfectly safe for downloading files) and restricted sites (which are likely to contain things that you wouldn't download to your worst enemy's computer).

Chapter
20

Get ready to . . .

Add or Change the Windows XP Password

1. Choose Start⇨Control Panel and then double-click User Accounts.

2. In the resulting window, click the Change an Account link. On the next screen, click an account to add the password to. Then click the Create a Password link.

3. In the Create a Password for Your Account screen, as shown in Figure 20-1, enter a password, confirm it, and add a password hint, if you wish.

4. Click the Create Password button.

5. You return to the User Accounts window and the What Do You Want to Change about Your Account? screen (see Figure 20-2). Here, you can click the Change My Password link, enter your old password, and then follow the procedure in Step 3 to change your password.

6. Click the Close button to close the User Accounts window.

 If you forget your password, Windows XP shows the hint you entered (see Step 3) to help you remember it. However, keep in mind that anybody who uses your computer can see the hint when it's displayed. So, if lots of people know that you drive a Ford and your hint is *My car model,* your password protection is about as effective as an umbrella in a monsoon.

 After you create a password, you may change your mind, for example you may move your computer to a more secure location and decide you don't need the password. You can go to the User Accounts window and remove the password by clicking the Remove My Password link.

Figure 20-1: The Create a Password for Your Account screen

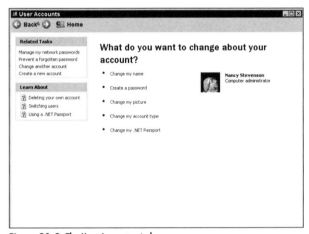

Figure 20-2: The User Accounts window

Use a Password-Protected Screen Saver

1. Choose Start➪Control Panel; click the Appearance and Themes link (see Figure 20-3), and click Choose a Screen Saver.

2. In the resulting Display Properties dialog box, click the Screen Saver tab, select the On Resume, Password Protect check box (see Figure 20-4), and then click OK. *Note:* If you're set up with multiple users, the selection here is On Resume, Display Welcome Screen.

3. When the screen saver activates, press a key or move your mouse to open the Display dialog box.

4. Enter your password (the one that you set up for Windows XP in the previous task) and then click OK.

 You can change settings for your screen saver by clicking the Settings button on the Screen Saver tab of the Display Properties dialog box. In the resulting dialog box, you can modify the style of the screen saver objects, the color scheme, and the size and resolution of the image.

 If you don't have a Windows XP password set and you activate the screen saver password feature, just click OK when you see the Display dialog box mentioned in Step 3. The screen saver password feature requires a password only if one is set up for Windows XP. Otherwise, the Display dialog box is all show!

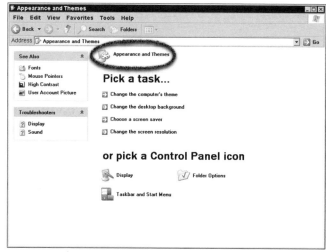

Figure 20-3: The Appearance and Themes dialog box

Figure 20-4: The Display Properties dialog box, Screen Saver tab

Use Shared Folders

1. Locate the folder that you want to share by using Windows Explorer. (Choose Start⇨All Programs⇨ Accessories⇨Windows Explorer.)

2. Click and drag the folder that you want to share to the Shared Documents folder in the Other Places pane on the left (see Figure 20-5).

3. Click the Shared Documents folder link in the left pane. The shared folder has been moved there where it is now available to others to use (see Figure 20-6).

 To find out more about using Windows Explorer to locate and work with files, see Chapter 10.

 You can right-click a file, choose Sharing and Security, and then use settings on the Sharing tab of the resulting dialog box to make a folder private on a standalone computer by selecting the Make this Folder Private check box. When you do, anyone logged in to your computer as another user can't access the folder.

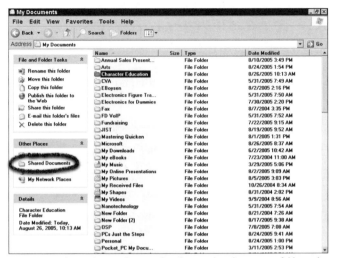

Figure 20-5: The Windows Explorer window showing Shared Documents folder in the Other Places pane

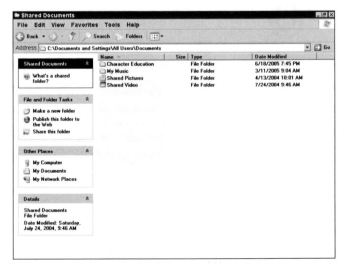

Figure 20-6: The contents of a Shared Documents folder

Set Up Trusted and Restricted Web Sites

1. Double-click the Internet Explorer icon on the Windows XP desktop to start the browser.

2. Choose Tools⇨Internet Options.

3. In the resulting Internet Options dialog box, click the Security tab (see Figure 20-7).

4. Click the Trusted Sites (or Restricted Sites) icon and then click the Sites button.

5. In the resulting Trusted Sites or Restricted Sites dialog box, enter a URL for a trusted Web site in the Add This Web Site to the Zone text box.

6. Click Add to add the site to the list of Web sites, as shown in Figure 20-8.

7. Repeat Steps 3–6 to add more trusted sites or restrict more untrusted sites.

8. When you're done, click OK twice to close the dialog boxes.

 Note that if the Require Server Verification (https:) for All Sites In This Zone check box is selected in the Trusted Sites dialog box, any Trusted site you add must use the `https` prefix, which indicates that the site has a secure connection.

 You can establish a Privacy setting on the Privacy tab of the Internet Options dialog box to control which sites are allowed to download cookies to your computer. *Cookies,* tiny files that are used to track your online activity, recognize you when you return to a source site. *Trusted sites* are the ones that you allow to download cookies to your computer even though the privacy setting you have made might not allow any other sites to do so. *Restricted sites* can never download cookies to your computer, no matter what your privacy setting is.

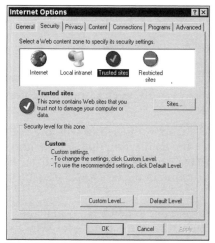

Figure 20-7: The Internet Options dialog box, Security tab

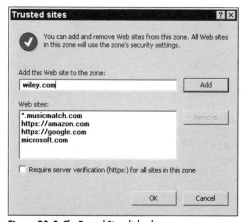

Figure 20-8: The Trusted Sites dialog box

Enable an Internet Connection Firewall

1. Choose Start⇨My Network Places.

2. In the Network Places window, click the View Network Connections link.

3. In the resulting Network Connections window (see Figure 20-9), click the connection that you want to protect in the right pane, and then click the Change Settings of This Connection link in the Network Task pane on the left.

4. In the resulting Properties dialog box, display the Advanced tab. Click the Settings button for Windows Firewall.

5. In the resulting Windows Firewall dialog box (see Figure 20-10) select the appropriate check box(es) to select connections you want to protect and then click OK.

 A *firewall* is a program that protects your computer from the outside world. This is generally a good thing unless you use a Virtual Private Network (VPN). Using a firewall with a VPN leaves you unable to share files and use some other VPN features.

 You can also choose Start⇨Control Panel⇨Security Center, and then click the Windows Firewall link to display the dialog box shown in Figure 20-10.

Figure 20-9: The Network Connections window

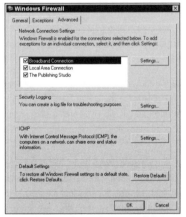

Figure 20-10: The Windows Firewall dialog box, Advanced tab

Install a Security Patch by Using Windows Update

1. Choose Start⇨All Programs⇨Windows Update.

2. In the Windows Update window, as shown in Figure 20-11, click the Express button. Windows XP thinks about this for a while, so feel free to flip through your junk mail for a minute or two.

3. A window might appear, asking you to download and install Windows XP components used to assist in your updating. Click Download and Install Now to proceed. You might also be asked to validate your copy of Windows XP, which simply checks that you have a legal copy of the software. Just follow instructions to do so, and you return to the Windows Update window.

4. After clicking the Express button, the Review and Install Updates window appears (see Figure 20-12).

5. Click the Install Updates button to install selected updates. The Installing Updates dialog box appears. Click the I Accept button, and the Installing Updates dialog box appears, showing you the download progress.

6. When the installation is complete, you see a message telling you that you must restart your computer to complete the installation. Click Restart Now to do so.

I recommend creating a system restore point just before downloading updates. Some updates can cause problems, and being able to restore your system back to the moment before their installation could save you heartache. See Chapter 22 for more about creating a system restore point.

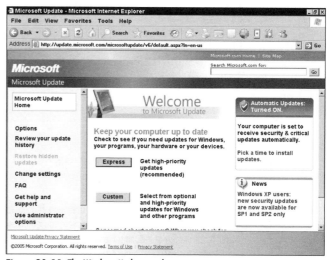

Figure 20-11: The Windows Update window

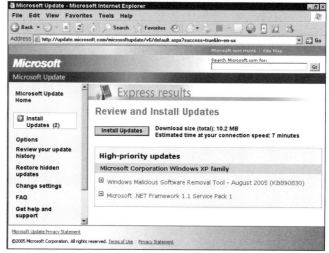

Figure 20-12: The Install Updates window

Set File Attributes

1. Locate the file that you want to modify by using Windows Explorer. (Choose Start➪All Programs➪Accessories➪ Windows Explorer.)

2. Right-click the file and choose Properties.

3. In the resulting *Filename* Properties dialog box, click the General tab (see Figure 20-13).

4. Select the Read-Only and/or Hidden check boxes.

5. Click OK to accept the new settings.

 The Advanced button next to the Read-Only and Hidden check boxes displays a dialog box that provides options for setting up the file for features such as including the file in indexing, which allows for faster file searches, and compressing the file to save disk space.

 If you want to see the files that you've marked as hidden, go to the file or folder location (for example, open the My Documents folder or use Windows Explorer) and choose Tools➪Folder Options. Click the View tab to display it. In the Advanced Settings area, select the Show Hidden Files and Folders option and then click OK.

Figure 20-13: The *Filename* Properties dialog box

Troubleshooting Hardware Problems

Computer hardware is stuff like your CPU and printer that takes up room on your desktop. Hardware gadgets make whirring noises and make use of your software so you can get your work done. But when your hardware isn't working, you might be tempted to drop-kick it into the trash. Don't do that — just think of all the money you spent on it. Instead, use Windows XP to isolate and troubleshoot the problem.

Windows XP has several features that help you diagnose and treat misbehaving hardware, including:

➡ A Printing Troubleshooter that walks you through a wizard-like interface to figure out what the printer problem is — and fix it.

➡ A Disk Defragmenter feature that checks your hard drive for problems that could be causing poor performance, such as bits of stray data that you could simply throw away, freeing up space and helping your system to perform better, or bad sectors on the drive.

➡ Modem diagnostics that analyze your modem to be sure that it's connected, configured, and performing properly.

➡ A Hardware Troubleshooter feature in the Windows Help and Support Center that walks you through choices to isolate and fix a variety of hardware problems.

➡ The ability to quickly and easily update hardware drivers that might help your hardware perform optimally or reinstall a corrupted driver.

Get ready to . . .

Troubleshoot a Printer Problem

1. Choose Start⇨Control Panel⇨Printers and Other Hardware⇨Printers and Faxes. In the window that appears, click the Printing link in the Troubleshooter area.

2. In the window that appears (see Figure 21-1), select the problem that's closest to what you're experiencing. For example, you're having trouble installing a local printer. Click Next.

3. What appears at this point differs depending on the printing problem that you're experiencing, but typically the Printing Troubleshooter gives you some instructions for procedures to try. So, for example, you might be told to

   • Try to print a test page and then select an option to tell the Troubleshooter that you can print from WordPad but not from the original application. (See Figure 21-2 for an example.)

   • Reinstall your printer driver.

   • Use TrueType fonts to format your document, which could stop your text from printing incorrectly.

4. Continue to try procedures and indicate the results, clicking Next to display the Troubleshooter's subsequent suggestions until you isolate and solve the problem.

5. Click the Close button in the upper-right corner to close the Troubleshooter.

 Here are some sneaky printer problems to look for: The printer isn't connected to the computer; the printer isn't plugged in; the printer driver is out of date; the printer doesn't have an ink cartridge in it; the printer isn't set up as the current printer (so you're printing to some other printer or trying to print to a printer that's no longer connected to your computer); or the printer lid is open.

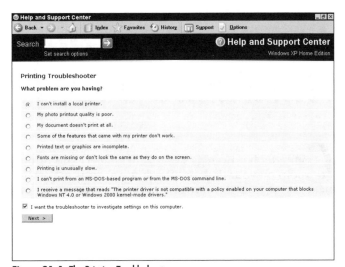

Figure 21-1: The Printing Troubleshooter

Figure 21-2: The Printing Troubleshooter in action

Use Disk Defragmenter to Check a Hard Drive for Errors

1. Choose Start⇨All Programs⇨Accessories⇨System Tools⇨ Disk Defragmenter.

2. In the Disk Defragmenter window (see Figure 21-3), click your hard drive (usually drive C) and then click the Analyze button. Disk Defragmenter analyzes the drive.

3. To view the resulting report (see Figure 21-4), click the View Report button in the dialog box that appears. Click the Close button to close the report. If the analysis recommends that you proceed, or if you just want to see what happens if you proceed, click the Defragment button. The procedure runs and cleans your hard drive, consolidating fragmented files to improve performance.

4. When Disk Defragmenter is finished, the Disk Defragmenter window closes.

Another tool that you can use to check your hard drive for potentially troublesome problems is Disk Cleanup. (Choose Start⇨All Programs⇨Accessories⇨System Tools⇨Disk Cleanup.) Disk Cleanup analyzes how much space you might save by getting rid of unused files and then offers you the option of getting rid of selected items. Clearing out unused files frees up hard drive space, which can allow your system to operate faster.

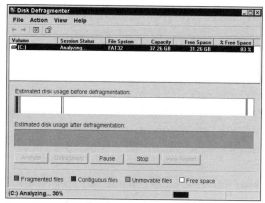

Figure 21-3: The Disk Defragmenter window

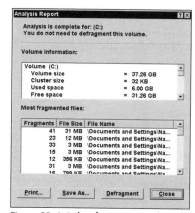

Figure 21-4: Disk Defragmenter's analysis of my hard drive

Run Error Checking to Detect Bad Sectors on a Hard Drive

1. Choose Start⇨My Computer.

2. Right-click the disk you want to repair and choose Properties from the menu that appears.

3. In the resulting Properties dialog box, click the Tools tab to display it (see Figure 21-5). Click the Check Now button.

4. In the resulting Check Disk dialog box (see Figure 21-6), choose the option you want to use:

- **Automatically Fix File System Errors:** *Note:* All files must be closed before you run this option.

- **Scan for and Attempt Recovery of Bad Sectors:** If you choose this, it also automatically fixes any file system errors found, so you don't need to mark the first option as well.

5. Click Start.

 If you attempt recovery of bad sectors, as the second option in Step 4 does, Windows XP may mark some sectors as unusable, in effect stopping any future use of those sectors. If you are concerned about marking bad sectors of your hard drive, stick to the first option, which simply repairs file errors.

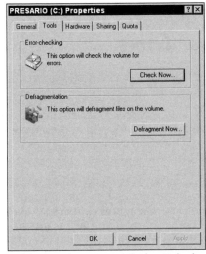

Figure 21-5: The Properties dialog box, Tools tab

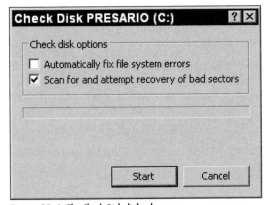

Figure 21-6: The Check Disk dialog box

Perform Modem Diagnostics

1. Choose Start⊏>Control Panel⊏>Printers and other Hardware⊏>Phone and Modem Options.

2. In the resulting dialog box (see Figure 21-7), click the Modems tab and then the Properties button. Click the Troubleshoot button on the Central tab of the Properties dialog box that appears.

3. In the resulting Modem Troubleshooter window (see Figure 21-8), select the description that best matches the problem that you're experiencing, and then click Next.

4. The information that appears differs depending on the modem problem you're experiencing, but typically the Modem Troubleshooter gives you some instructions for procedures to try. (See Figure 21-8 for an example.)

5. Click Next to proceed through these screens until you isolate the problem.

6. Click the Close button in the upper-right corner of the Troubleshooter to close it.

When using any Windows XP troubleshooter, I recommend leaving the I Want the Troubleshooter to Investigate Settings on this Computer check box in the initial window selected. This doesn't open you up to anybody on the Internet coming in and looking over your system; it simply allows the troubleshooter to check certain settings within your system. This is faster than having to check them yourself, so it's a good thing to do.

Figure 21-7: The Phone and Modem dialog box, Modem tab

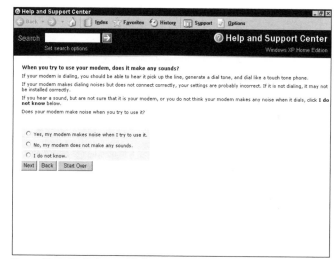

Figure 21-8: The Modem Troubleshooter

Use the Hardware Troubleshooter

1. Choose Start⇨Help and Support⇨Hardware⇨Fixing a Hardware Problem⇨Hardware Troubleshooter.

2. In the resulting Hardware Troubleshooter window, as shown in Figure 21-9, select the item that most closely matches the problem that you're having and then click Next.

3. In the resulting window, follow the instructions that relate to your problem. (Figure 21-10 shows instructions for a display adapter problem as an example.)

4. If the resulting information solves the problem, select Yes, This Solves the Problem. Select No, I Still Have a Problem if the information doesn't help. Click Next.

5. After you solve the problem, click the Close button to close the Hardware Troubleshooter.

 If you're following the Hardware Troubleshooter and decide that you've taken the wrong path somewhere or should have tried an alternate suggested procedure, quickly go back and start again by clicking the Start Over button on any Troubleshooter screen. You can also go back, screen by screen, by clicking the Back button.

 Occasionally, you see a link in a troubleshooter window that takes you to a different troubleshooter. For example, if you started to troubleshoot a CD drive and indicate you could use data files but not play audio files from the drive, a Sound Troubleshooter link might be available. However, if you follow this link, you leave the troubleshooter you're in and have to start it again if the new option is a dead end.

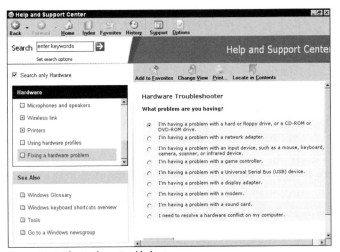

Figure 21-9: The Hardware Troubleshooter

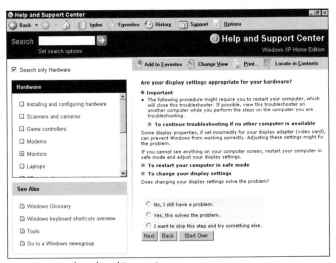

Figure 21-10: The Help and Support Center

Update a Driver

1. Put the CD or floppy disk with the updated driver on it in the appropriate drive of your computer, or download a driver onto your hard drive from the Internet.

2. Choose Start➪Control Panel➪Performance and Maintenance➪System.

3. In the resulting System Properties dialog box, click the Hardware tab to display it and then click the Device Manager button (see Figure 21-11).

4. In the resulting window, click the plus sign next to any hardware item to display the installed hardware, and then click a hardware item and choose Action➪Update Driver from the menu bar.

5. In the resulting Hardware Update Wizard window (see Figure 21-12), you can choose to:

- **Install the driver automatically.** This sends Windows XP scurrying around your hard drive to locate it.

- **Install it from a specific source, such as a CD-ROM.** The next window that appears provides ways to search removable media such as a floppy disk or CD, or to specify a location on your computer.

6. Follow the rest of the steps indicated by the wizard based on your choices to update your driver. When the wizard is done, click Finish.

 In some cases, you have to reboot your computer to give Windows XP a chance to load the new driver. Choose Start➪Turn Off Computer. In the resulting Turn Off Computer dialog box, click the Restart button to reboot your system. The driver should now, by the magic of the Windows Plug and Play feature that automatically detects new hardware, be working.

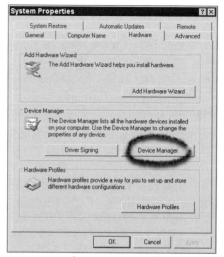

Figure 21-11: The System Properties dialog box

Figure 21-12: The Hardware Update Wizard

Reinstall a Corrupted Driver

1. Locate the device associated with the corrupted driver, turn off the device, and disconnect it from your computer.

2. Choose Start⇨Control Panel⇨Performance and Maintenance⇨System.

3. In the System Properties dialog box, click the Hardware tab (see Figure 21-13) and then click the Device Manager button.

4. In the resulting window (see Figure 21-14), choose the category relating to your device. Right-click the specific device and then choose Uninstall from the pop-up menu.

5. When the uninstall procedure is complete, restart your computer, reconnect the device, and turn it on. At this point, you can do a couple of things to reinstall the driver:

   • Insert a disc containing the driver and run the installation from that disc. This usually involves double-clicking a `setup.exe` file from Windows Explorer.

   • Allow the Plug and Play feature of Windows XP to automatically detect and install the driver for you.

 If Plug and Play doesn't install the driver automatically and you don't have it on a disk/c, you can use the Add Hardware Wizard to install it. Choose Start⇨Control Panel⇨Add Hardware to call up the Add Hardware Wizard.

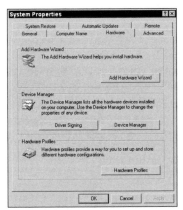

Figure 21-13: The System Properties dialog box, Hardware tab

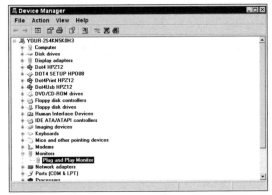

Figure 21-14: The Device Manager window

Troubleshooting Software Problems

All the bells and whistles on your computer hardware won't do you much good if the software driving it isn't working properly. If any programs cause your system to *crash* (freezing up so your screen just sits there staring at you and ignoring mouse clicks and keystrokes for all its worth), you can try a variety of tasks to fix it. In this chapter, you find out how to recover when the following software problems occur:

➡ When a program crashes, you can simply shut that program down by using the Windows Task Manager. This utility keeps track of all programs and processes running on your computer.

➡ If you've got problems and Windows XP isn't responding, restart in Safe Mode, which requires only basic files and drivers and often allows you to troubleshoot the problem. You can restart Windows XP in its regular mode after you fix things.

➡ Use the System Restore feature to first create a *system restore point* (a time when your settings and programs were working just fine) and then restore Windows XP to that point when trouble hits.

➡ If all else fails, *reformat* an entire drive. This wipes all information from the drive; if it's the hard drive that you reformat, you have to start again by reloading the operating system and all software.

Get ready to . . .

Shut Down a Non-Responsive Application

1. Press Ctrl+Alt+Delete.

2. In the Windows Task Manager dialog box (see Figure 22-1), select the application that you were in when your system stopped responding.

3. Click the End Task button.

4. In the resulting dialog box (see Figure 22-2), the Windows Task Manager tells you that the application isn't responding and asks whether you want to shut it down now. Click the End Now button.

 If pressing Ctrl+Alt+Delete doesn't bring up the Task Manager, you might be in bigger trouble than you thought. You can press Ctrl+Alt+Del twice at any time, and Windows XP reboots. If this doesn't work simply press and hold the power button on your computer to reboot. Sometimes rebooting by either method solves the problem, and you can get right back to work. Note that some applications use an Auto Recover feature that keeps an interim version of the document that you were working in; you might be able to save some of your work by opening that last-saved version. Other programs don't have such a safety net, and you simply lose whatever changes you made to your document since the last time you last saved it. The moral? Save, and save often.

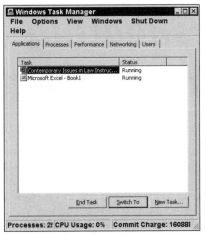

Figure 22-1: The Windows Task Manager

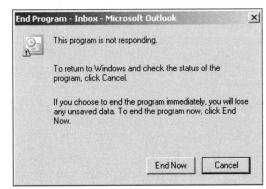

Figure 22-2: A non-responsive program message

Start Windows XP in Safe Mode

1. Choose Start⇨Turn Off Computer. In the Turn Off Computer dialog box (see Figure 22-3), click the Restart button to reboot your system.

2. When the computer starts to reboot (the screen goes black), begin pressing F8 repeatedly.

3. When the plain vanilla text-based screen appears, press the up- or down-arrow key to select the Safe Mode option from the list and then press Enter.

4. On the resulting screen, use the up- and down-arrow keys to select the Windows XP operating system. Or, type the number of that choice. Then press Enter.

5. In the resulting dialog box, which explains what Safe Mode is and gives the option of running System Restore, click Yes to open Windows XP Safe Mode, as shown in Figure 22-4.

6. Use the tools in Control Panel and the Help and Support system to figure out your problem, make changes, and then restart. When you restart again (repeat Step 1), you start in the standard Windows XP mode.

 When you reboot and press F8 as in Step 2, you're in the old text-based world that users of DOS remember. It's scary out there — your mouse doesn't work a lick, and no fun sounds or cool graphics exist to soothe you. In fact, DOS is the reason the whole *For Dummies* series started because *everybody* felt like a dummy using it, me included. Just use your arrow keys to get around and press Enter to make selections. You're back in Windows-land soon.

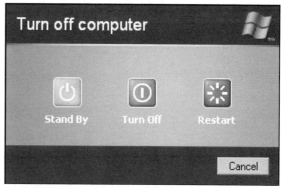

Figure 22-3: The Turn Off Computer dialog box

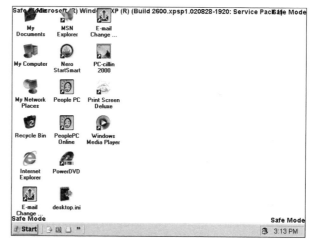

Figure 22-4: Windows XP running in Safe Mode

Create a System Restore Point

1. Choose Start⇨All Programs⇨Accessories⇨System Tools⇨ System Restore.

2. Select the Create a Restore Point radio button and then click Next.

3. In the resulting dialog box (see Figure 22-5), fill in the Restore Point Description text box; a description such as "Before installing Service Pack 2" is helpful if you create multiple restore points and want to identify the correct one. The current date is usually your best bet.

4. Click the Create button, and the system restore point is created and is available to you when you run a System Restore (see Figure 22-6).

 Every once in a while, when things seem to be running just fine — especially before you install some software and make some new settings in Windows XP — create a system restore point. It's good computer practice, just like backing up your files, only you're backing up your settings. Once a month or once every couple months works for most people, but if you frequently make changes, create a system restore point more often.

 A more drastic option to System Restore is to run the system recovery disc that probably came with your computer. However, system recovery essentially puts your computer right back to the configuration it had when it was shipped from the factory. That means you lose any software you've installed and documents you've created since you began to use it. A good argument for creating system restore points on a regular basis, don't you think?

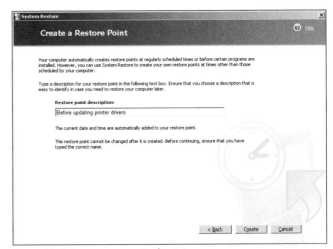

Figure 22-5: A system restore point description

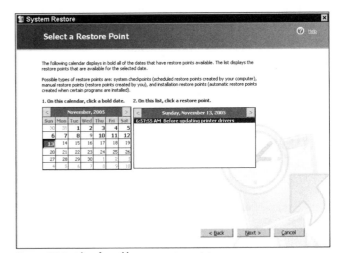

Figure 22-6: A list of possible system restore points

Restore the Windows XP System

1. Choose Start➪All Programs➪Accessories➪System Tools➪ System Restore.

2. In the System Restore dialog box (see Figure 22-7), accept the default option of Restore My Computer to an Earlier Time by clicking Next.

3. In the resulting dialog box, click the arrow keys on the right or left of the calendar to search the months and locate the system restore point that you want to use. (Refer to Figure 22-6.)

4. Select the system restore point that you want to use and then click Next.

5. As prompted by the Confirm System Restore Point Selection dialog box, as shown in Figure 22-8, shut down any running programs. When you're ready, click Next.

6. The system goes through a shutdown and restart sequence, and then displays a dialog box that informs you that the System Restore has occurred.

7. Click OK to close it.

 System Restore doesn't get rid of files that you've saved, so you don't lose your long-awaited first novel. System Restore simply reverts to Windows settings as of the Restore Point. This can help if you — or some piece of software you installed — make a setting that causes some conflict in your system that makes your computer sluggish or prone to crashes.

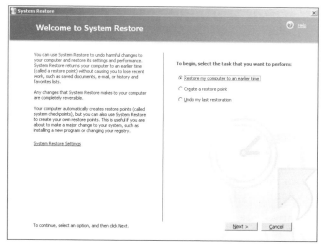

Figure 22-7: The Welcome to System Restore dialog box

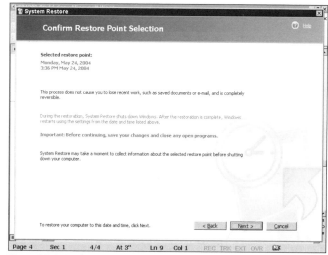

Figure 22-8: Ready to run a System Restore

Reformat a Drive

1. Assuming your system is still functional enough to let you do so, back up everything you can find (documents, photos, graphics, saved e-mails, updates, drivers, and so on) and close all applications. *Hint:* Don't worry about software programs because you'll have to reinstall those, anyway.

2. Choose Start⇨Control Panel⇨Performance and Maintenance⇨Administrative Tools.

3. In the Administrative Tools window (see Figure 22-9), double-click the Computer Management link.

4. In the resulting Computer Management window (see Figure 22-10), choose Disk Management (in the left pane). Right-click the drive or partition that you want to reformat (in the right pane) and then choose Format from the shortcut menu that appears.

5. In the resulting dialog box, select the options you want and then click OK.

 You have to be logged on as the head honcho — the system administrator — to perform these steps. And it's worth repeating: Reformatting a drive wipes *everything* off it, so be sure that's what you want to do before you do it.

 I can't stress this strongly enough: Before you reformat a drive, you should back up everything you can, including drivers or updates to software that you've sat through tedious minutes (or hours) to download from the Web. You don't want to have to spend all that download time all over again to get yourself up to speed. This goes double if you installed Windows Service Pack 2: If you've gone through the few hours it takes to download and install, I'm sure you'll agree that once was enough! Also always keep your Windows XP installation CD handy; if Windows XP was preinstalled on your computer, make system backup CDs or DVDs and keep them nearby.

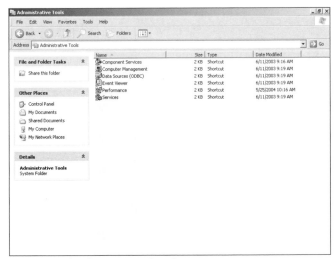

Figure 22-9: The Administrative Tools window

 Backing up files before running any system maintenance procedure is a good idea. Better safe than sorry. For more about how to back up files, see Chapter 8.

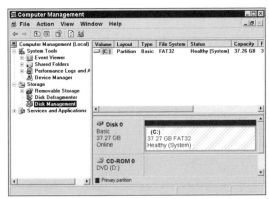

Figure 22-10: The Computer Management window

➤ Index

• H •

hard drive
  bad sectors, 212
  error checking, 211
  initializing new, 66
  properties, 14
  reformatting, 222
hardware troubleshooting
  Disk Defragmenter and, 211
  driver updates, 215
  error checking hard drive, 212
  hard drive bad sectors, 212
  Hardware Troubleshooter, 214
  modem diagnostics, 213
  printers, 210
Help
  Remote Assistance, 90–91
  searches, 89
  topics, 88
Hibernate setting, laptops, 40
history, Web browsing, 156
home page setup, 153

• I •

icons, desktop, arranging, 53
images, desktop, 110
imaging devices, installation, 131
input devices
  game controllers, 17, 21
  keyboard, 17, 20
  keyboard, options, 27
  mouse, 17, 19

Plug and Play, 18
  Table PC and, 18
  types, 18
  wireless devices, 18
inserting
  CD-ROMs, 12
  DVDs, 12
installation
  graphics card, 106
  hard drive, initialization, 66
  imaging devices, 131
  memory cards, 65
  printers, 30–31
  scanners, 37
  security patches, 207
  software, 69
installed printers, viewing, 33
Internet Connection Firewall, enabling, 206
Internet connections
  always-on, setup, 144
  default, 146
  removing, 147
  repairing, 147
  setup, 140
  sharing, 142
  TCP/IP, 143
Internet Explorer
  Content Advisor, 159
  customization, 157
  privacy settings, 158
ISPs
  connection setup, 140
  dial-up connection, new, 141

• J •

joysticks, introduction, 17

• K •

keyboard, on-screen, 28
Keyboard Properties dialog box
  repeat delay, 27
  setup, 19
keyboards
  input options, 27
  introduction, 17
  setup, 19
  uses, 18

• L •

laptops
  battery power, 40
  briefcase, creating, 43
  briefcase, synchronizing files, 44
  file sharing, 39
  Hibernate setting, 40
  low power alarm, 42
  power management, 39
  power options, 40
  speaker connection, 6
  Standby, manual selection, 41
local area connection, networking, 182
log off Windows XP, 48
log on to Windows XP, 48
log-on screen, Windows XP, 7
low battery alarm, laptops, 42

• M •

Magnifier, 25
Map Network Drive dialog box, 193
mapping, folders to drive, 193
media drives, 11. *See also* drives; storage
Media Player, 123, 128
memory
  adding, 65
  cards, installation, 65
  Disk Defragmenter and, 64
  freeing, 63
  installed, checking, 62
  overview, 61
  partitioning disks and, 66
menus, All Programs, 49
message folders, Outlook, 172–173
messages, Outlook Express. *See* Outlook Express
Messenger, contacts, 99
modem diagnostics, 213
monitor
  DPI setting, 107
  drivers, updating, 105
  refresh rate, 108
  resolution, 109
Monitor Properties dialog box, 104
monitors
  enabling, 104
  speaker connection, 6
motherboard, introduction, 11
mouse
  introduction, 17
  setup, 19
  uses, 18

• V •

video effects in movies, 130
Video Effects pane, 130
voice options, Narrator, 26
Voice Settings dialog box (Narrator), 26
volume, 118

• W •

Web
  browsing history, 156
  file downloads, 158
  Internet Explorer, customization, 157
  navigating, 150
  searching, 151
Web pages
  home page setup, 153
  printing, 160
  searching, 152
Web sites
  adding to Favorites, 154
  restricted, 205
  trusted, 205
windows
  applications windows, resizing, 51
  applications windows, switching between, 51
  Performance and Maintenance, 40

Windows Explorer, Folders, 77
Windows Movie Maker, project creation, 129
Windows Picture and Fax Viewer, digital image
    viewing, 132
Windows Scanner and Camera Wizard, 135
Windows Sound Recorder, 125
Windows Update, 92
  running, 72
  security patch installation, 207
Windows XP
  closing applications, 50
  color scheme, 113
  components, adding/removing, 71
  desktop navigation, 9
  introduction, 47
  log on/off, 48
  log-on screen, 7
  opening applications, 49
  password, 202
  restoring system, 221
  turn off PC, 8
wireless devices, input and, 18
Wireless Network Setup Wizard, 186
wireless networks, configuration, 186
WordPad, document creation, 93
workgroups
  joining, 188
  viewing computers on, 189